Social Psychology: A Very Short Introduction

VERY SHORT INTRODUCTIONS are for anyone wanting a stimulating and accessible way into a new subject. They are written by experts, and have been translated into more than 40 different languages.

The series began in 1995, and now covers a wide variety of topics in every discipline. The VSI library now contains over 400 volumes—a Very Short Introduction to everything from Psychology and Philosophy of Science to American History and Relativity—and continues to grow in every subject area.

Very Short Introductions available now:

Available soon:

For more information visit our website

www.oup.com/vsi/

Richard J. Crisp

SOCIAL PSYCHOLOGY

A Very Short Introduction

OXFORD
UNIVERSITY PRESS

Great Clarendon Street, Oxford, OX2 6DP,
United Kingdom

Oxford University Press is a department of the University of Oxford.
It furthers the University's objective of excellence in research, scholarship,
and education by publishing worldwide. Oxford is a registered trade mark of
Oxford University Press in the UK and in certain other countries

Published in the United States of America by Oxford University Press
198 Madison Avenue, New York, NY 10016, United States of America

British Library Cataloguing in Publication Data
Data available

Library of Congress Control Number: 2015933891

ISBN 978-0-19-871551-1

Printed in Great Britain by
Ashford Colour Press Ltd., Gosport, Hampshire.

Contents

List of illustrations

Chapter 1
All about us

Science is often considered a quest to understand the physical universe: How atoms, molecules, and materials interact to determine our fate. Yet to the *social* scientist, understanding how we live, work, and co-exist with one another is as important as understanding the physical world. It is this 'social universe' that defines who we are, what we achieve, and what we leave behind.

Social psychology is all about this social universe, and the people who populate our everyday lives. It's the study of how society, culture, and context shape attitudes, behaviour, and beliefs. It's about how we figure out who we are, and how this is intimately linked to our relationships with others. It's about families, neighbours, co-workers, lovers, enemies, politicians, soap stars, sports stars, and strangers. Social psychology is all about us, and it's what this book is all about.

In what follows, I'll tell the story of social psychology; its history, pivotal moments, and major theories. I'll show you the classic studies that have defined the discipline to date. I'll talk about key thinkers, and how their personal histories spurred them to understand what connects people to people, and to the societies in which we live. I'll talk about the groundbreaking research that's made social psychology one of the most important and engaging disciplines of our time. From attitudes to attraction, prejudice to persuasion, health to happiness, social psychology provides insights that can change the world, and help tackle the defining problems of the 21st century.

So lets start with a little bit of history, and how the discipline came to be.

The early years

From Aristotle's ancient philosophizing, to the works of economists like Marx and Engle, to the sociological theories of Durkheim, understanding the nature of human society has been an enduring scholarly pursuit. It wasn't, however, until sometime around the middle of the 19th century that social psychology (as we know it today) came in to being. It was a natural integration of ideas that emerged as philosophers, sociologists, anthropologists, and academics from many other disciplines began to ask: how do individual hopes, aspirations, and abilities shape our relations with others? How do individuals influence their groups, organizations, and society at large? In turn, how does society affect individuals' thoughts, feelings, and, ultimately, their behaviour?

Gustav LeBon, a French sociologist, anthropologist, inventor, and physicist, is widely regarded as having established the first truly psychological thesis on society. In his 1885 book *The Crowd: A Study of the Popular Mind*, LeBon proposed the idea of the 'crowd mind'. This was an inspired, and completely new, way of thinking about human behaviour. LeBon argued that people do not have fixed, unchanging capacities for good and evil. Instead, he proposed that in the presence of others our individuality can be transmuted in to a 'collective mind'. Sounds far-fetched? Well, that's probably how it was perceived at the time, but it's not so far from what we now know goes on in collectivist animal species like ants or bees. LeBon argued that people's behaviour in a crowd triggers something akin to what is observed in the animal kingdom, a group with a mind of its own that suppresses each individual's attitudes, values, and beliefs. This was a simple and controversial idea—that individuals may experience a 'diffusion of responsibility' for their actions in the presence of others. It was also a dramatic departure from basic assumptions in related branches of social science, most notably economics. The notion that people are not always rational, and can behave in ways that are patently out of line with their privately held beliefs, was a fundamental challenge to the predominant view of human ascendancy. As we will see later on, this idea proved pivotal to some of social psychology's most influential research on attitude formation and change.

LeBon's theory was a major theoretical and epistemological development, but what came next was to further define the emergence of this new science. An essential element of contemporary social psychology is its focus on testable theory, hypothesis generation, and adherence to the experimental methods espoused in the natural sciences. The origins of this approach lie in 1898 with what is arguably the first social psychological experiment, carried out by Norman Triplett at Indiana University. Triplett was interested in crowds, just like LeBon. However, he focused not on the negative effects of social influence, but on the positive effects of being in a collective. Triplett had noticed that sometimes, in the presence of others, people performed better at whatever task they do, be this athletics, music, or at work. What he wanted to do was find a way of quantifying this apparent uplift in performance in an objective, measureable way. He therefore gave a group of children a simple game to play. In this game the aim was to turn a fishing reel as quickly as possible. Importantly, Triplett compared the children's performance under two different task conditions: either alone or in pairs. What he found was that when the children performed in pairs they turned the fishing reels far more quickly than when they were asked to do the task alone. This was the first documented case of a scientific experiment in psychology, and it revealed an enduring phenomenon that is still the source of intense study today. I'll talk about this intriguing effect more in Chapter 3.

A sign that any new discipline has come of age is the production of a textbook, and the start of the 20th century saw the arrival of two on social psychology. In the UK, in 1908, William McDougall authored *An Introduction to Social Psychology* while in 1924 US psychologist Floyd Allport authored *Social Psychology*. Both of these books built on Triplett's pioneering work to cement the discipline as an experimental science.

McDougall's book was very much rooted in biology—he conceptualized social behaviour as driven by inherited or innate characteristics. Allport's book relied less on creating an intellectual grounding in the natural sciences, and more on adapting their methods. He advocated the adoption of objectivity and experimental control, calling for a 'hard science' approach to the study of human behaviour. He pushed the discipline further from its sociological roots to focus much more on individuals as the agents of social change, coining terms that are still used to this day (such as 'social facilitation' and 'conformity').

The war years

During the 1930s and 1940s research on social psychology underwent an exponential growth in popularity. Numerous studies began to emerge from both the US and across Europe. New phenomena were discovered with increasing frequency, ranging from LaPierre's 'Attitudes vs. Actions' study of 1934, to Sherif's social influence research in 1935, to Hovland and Sear's 1940 work on aggression. I'll cover these classic studies in detail later on so won't provide any spoilers just yet. What is important here is that this activity in the 1930s and 1940s came to define the discipline for the next fifty years—it was a true age of discovery for social psychology.

Why this explosion of activity? The answer lies in the unrest and tragic events that engulfed the world during the first half of the 20th century. After two world wars, scientists turned their attention to the study of human behaviour with increasing vigour and urgency. Social psychology had become not just an interesting intellectual pursuit; it was suddenly critical to understanding the nature of human conflict and aggression.

Imagine yourself a social scientist, there in the late 1940s, at the dawn of the Cold War. Living with the very real prospect of nuclear annihilation. What would you do? Arguably it was not technological advances, in physics, chemistry, and engineering, that were the cause of war (these just made it easier and faster for us to kill each other). The cause of war lay within human nature, and our capacity to create intractable divides, seemingly solved only in conflict.

With technologies accelerating at an unprecedented pace, the urgency of understanding how humans relate to one another, in cooperation, conciliation, and conflict, became gravely important. It was therefore imperative that advances in social psychology keep up with advances in engineering and the physical sciences. If not, our capacity for conflict would rapidly surpass our capacity for peaceful coexistence. As we will see, the two world wars provided inspiration for many of the studies that came to shape the field of social psychology as it is today.

The cognitive revolution

In the 1980s the advent of modern computing did more than just transform the speed and efficiency with which scientists could analyse data; for psychologists it also provided a metaphor for the internal workings of the human mind. Understanding the ways that computers encode, organize, process, and output data provided a new template for cognitive psychologists, one that was readily adopted by social psychologists as well.

For instance, behaviour was thought to be the result of an input–compute–output process. So, a positive impression would be formed of someone if a higher proportion of positive to negative behaviours were computed from the available data. Social cognition, as it became known, emerged as a core element of theory and research spanning the different topics that comprise social psychology. The field moved away from the behaviourism-inspired approaches of the preceding decades. It aimed to not only predict behaviour, but to understand the inner workings of the 'social mind'. It aimed to build theory that directly addressed how our attitudes, beliefs, values, and ideologies were represented, and how these representations could change, interact, and predict behaviour. In 1991 Fiske and Taylor published a book called *Social Cognition* that summed up this new approach, and it is still core to many social psychology university reading lists today.

Of course, computers didn't only provide a new way of thinking about how people process information about other people, they also spawned a whole new approach to experimentation and data collection. Up until then the main way of measuring attitudes and behaviour was through observation, quantitative approaches (questionnaires and numerical scales), or qualitative approaches (interviews, textual analysis, and discourse). Computers provided the means to both present stimuli, and measure attitudes, at the millisecond response time level.

This was important because it enabled researchers to assess the influence of social stimuli perceived outside of conscious awareness (e.g. by presenting words like 'male', 'female', 'young', or 'old' on a computer faster than the eye can detect—around 300 milliseconds—but still fast enough for the brain to register). This allowed researchers to examine the more subtle effects of social environment on behaviour, and also helped them get around the problem of people giving socially desirable responses, rather than reporting their 'true' attitude. One of the things we have learned about people is they often don't say exactly what they think (especially when in the presence of others, or when their responses will be scrutinized by others). Response time methodologies allowed researchers to assess people's real, underlying attitude, free from the shackles of social norms and self-regulation.

Cognition in context

While pivotal to the development of the discipline, some have argued that the cognitive revolution initially focused disproportionately on the internal workings of the social mind, and to an extent ignored the effects of social context. To remedy this, in recent years there has been an increasing focus on so-called 'situated cognition'; that is, the way in which social cognition is affected and impacted by social context. The most important theoretical shift has been from the notion that cognitive processes are fixed and invariable, to instead embrace the idea that cognition is an emergent property of the situation at hand. In other words, how people think in social contexts is not a product of stored, static representations or learned rules, but can change fundamentally depending upon context and frame of reference.

For instance, rather than people having a single stereotype stored in memory that they apply to everyone they meet from a particular social group (e.g. Muslims), their expectations about meeting different members of that group will differ depending on their relationships (e.g. a friend and neighbour versus a stranger) and context (e.g. at home versus at work). The importance of context and relationships to how people construct a sense of their social worlds is now a strong theme in social psychology and something we'll discuss through all the chapters that follow.

Social psychology today

Social psychology is now a global endeavour, researched in many different laboratories around the world. Social psychological research is published in over one hundred journals, and new findings reported in newspapers on a daily basis. The Social Psychology Network (an educational organization with more than 2,000 members worldwide) has had its web pages viewed hundreds of millions of times since its founding in 1996.

Whether we are talking about research on obedience, conformity, prejudice, or persuasion, studies of social psychology have provided a range of important insights for business, governments, charities, and other organizations. Attitudes, leadership, tolerance, aggression, affiliation and attraction, friendship and love—these are concepts that have broad practical relevance for a range of careers and occupations, from management to education, health to the arts, government to the media. Social psychology is a discipline with incredible versatility, applicability, and relevance to the modern world. In this book I hope to give you a firm footing in the field as you adapt, use, and apply its insights in your own social universe.

Chapter 2
The social mind

This chapter is all about the basic workings of the social mind—in other words, social *cognition*. Cognition refers to the mechanics of thinking—it's how we perceive, process, retain, and recall information. For example, while you are reading this sentence your brain is engaging a whole range of mechanisms. First you are seeing the words. This visual input is then translated, encoded, and matched to a memory for what those words mean. As you access each word's meaning it is compiled in to a sentence structure according to other stored rules. The sentence is interpreted and kept in working memory so it can assist the processing of the next sentence, then the next paragraph, and ultimately the chapter. Finally, the key information is summarized, abstracted, and stored for assistance in interpreting subsequent information.

Social cognition works in much the same way—except the stimuli, meaning and, interpretation is all about the content of our social universe. Social cognition is therefore about how we encode, analyse, store, and use information about the people we meet and the relationships that define us. It is about the mental processes that 'kick in' as soon as we communicate with someone else. It is the nuts and bolts of social psychology, and forms the basis for pretty much everything I'll talk about in this book.

So what is social cognition in practice? Well, we're doing it all the time, we just don't realize it. Think, for example, about what mental processes will be initiated when you wake up tomorrow morning. Perhaps you'll start off thinking about that presentation you have to prepare for later in the day. Why do you want to prepare for it? Well, there are explicit rules—it's what your boss has told you to do. But there are also implicit rules—rules we don't see but which exert a powerful effect on our behaviour. You won't want to look stupid in front of your colleagues (and that's a *social* influence). Then there's the bigger picture—you want to do a good job to progress in your career. Why do you want to do this? It's key to your aspirations, and you want to make your friends and family proud (self-esteem, social comparison—they're *social* processes).

Ok, perhaps you're not thinking about that but listening to the radio. The DJ is engaged in a humorous segment about a trip she made to the supermarket (the fruit stand crashes down when she reaches out to take a peach). Why are you laughing? You're empathizing with the DJ (a social connection) and recognizing the situation (embarrassment in front of *others*—another *social* process).

On the other hand perhaps you're heading downstairs to breakfast. The whole family is there. Your dad starts asking you about your schoolwork (social pressure from a significant other), you're still a bit annoyed with your sister after a fight yesterday (an interpersonal relation), and you're not eating bacon because you saw a documentary last week about how animals are slaughtered (attitude change).

I could go on. At pretty much every point in our day social cognition is in effect. Even when we're alone, we're thinking about others. Why was your boyfriend distant this morning? Will my boss support my promotion application? Every person we know or meet stimulates the social mind. And none of this is to mention the big issues in the news. Immigration, politics, economics—there are social issues and influences that surround us each and every day.

Cognition lies at the heart of this social influence; it drives our attitudes and prejudices, our altruism and aggression. In this chapter I'll cover the basics of social cognition, and in particular how we form impressions of others. To do that, I need to go right back to the beginnings of social psychology, and a metaphor that was to define the early days of the discipline.

The naïve scientist

Pioneering social psychologist Fritz Heider wanted to build a basic theory of the social mind, and to do that he aimed to establish the fundamental guiding principles that drive social behaviour. The idea was that while people, like animals, had a hierarchy of survival needs (with basic needs like food, sleep, and sex at the top), we also have some essential epistemological and existential needs. Our complex minds need to know who we are, and how the world works, in order to survive.

Heider's view was that we are not simply passive observers of our worlds, but that we constantly encode, analyse, and process social information because it helps us meet two fundamental needs. The first is the need to *understand* the world and the second is to try to *control* it. In other words, human behaviour is driven by the need to predict and control.

These drives make perfect evolutionary sense. The success of any organism depends precisely upon these two principles: the ability to process information that enables the building of lay theories about the world, and basing an understanding about the working of that world on learning principles that enable prediction. If we can understand the world and predict what happens within it, we can control it; and if we can control it, we can survive (and pass on our genes). So for our human ancestors, it was adaptive to understand that tigers were to be avoided, while goats were good to herd. The point is that these principles apply to social relations too. Learning which people and which 'tribes' were aggressive, and so which to avoid, would have kept our ancestors safe, secure, and able to thrive.

Heider believed that this need to construct a working model of the world was so deep that we seek meaning and intention in all interactions—whether social or non-social. In a classic study he demonstrated this fundamental drive. Heider and Marianne Simmel, in their article 'An experimental study of apparent behavior', played a group of participants a short film that featured a number of small shapes (i.e. triangles and circles) moving in and around a large square (with an opening on one side). After watching this very simple animation participants were asked to respond to just one question: 'what did you see?'

Heider and Simmel found that only *one* person in the study described precisely what they had seen (i.e. 'A large triangle enters a rectangle and moves around'). All the other participants described—and interpreted—what occurred as the actions of *people*. For example, one response was: 'A man has planned to meet a girl and the girl comes along with another man. The first man tells the second to go. The second man shakes his head. Then the two men have a fight.' In other words, the participants had built a meaning system around what they saw—seeing the shapes as representing people, and matching the movements they observed as being representative of patterns of social interaction.

What Heider uncovered here was a fundamental human desire to want things to *just make sense*, one that defines the way in which the social mind processes information. According to Heider, this core need to understand the world about us shapes how we collect and process information, in particular about the people who populate our social universe. He argued that we are basically 'naïve scientists', building mental models to represent how the world works. As discussed in Chapter 1, before the science of psychology came into being the prevailing view of human nature held by other social scientists was that humans are rational, analytical, and logical. According to Heider these qualities are simply manifestations of the mind of the naïve scientist: we want to make sense of the world, and are constantly seeking to encode, analyse, and classify the movements of others. Working out how the social mind does this was to inspire the development of a major area of research in social psychology: attribution theory.

Attribution theory

Attribution is what we do to make sense of the world. It is how we make inferences about the causes of people's behaviour. We make attributions every day, they are how we ascertain *cause and effect* in our social universe. Imagine you walk down the corridor at work and see two of your friends arguing. What thoughts go through your mind? You're probably not looking at what they're wearing. You're probably engaging in a process of attribution—to try to work out why they are fighting. In other words, you're trying to *attribute* a cause to the effect (what has *caused* the arguing).

Take another example—that boy or girl you like keeps looking over at you. Think about the thoughts going through your head at that moment. Is it because they like you too, or are you imagining it? In this instance you're trying to infer something about their intentions from their behaviour—you're trying to attribute a *cause* (preferably that they like you too) to the *effect* (them looking over at you).

Despite its rather technical sounding name, attribution is as everyday a theory as there is. We literally do it all the time, even when trying to work out our own needs, desires, and drives ('do I want to study psychology at university? I seem to enjoy it, except the statistics, etc. . . .').

So making attributions is a key aspect of social cognition, how we determine cause and effect in our social universe. However, there is an important difference between calculating cause and effect in our social universe compared to the physical universe. Physical objects don't change in the light of the situation (unless we get in to quantum physics, but lets stay with basic Newtonian mechanics for now!). On the other hand, social objects do.

Take a pen. A pen is a pen whatever the situation, wherever it is. The defining characteristics of a pen do not change whether it's in your pocket, in your hand, or on the table. Determining why a pen produces ink is easy; there is a stable cause and a stable effect, regardless of context.

Now take a person. People have defining characteristics—their personalities. However, while these personalities are relatively stable they do change depending upon the situation. You will act differently when you're with your friends compared to when you're in a job interview. To understand and predict people we cannot ignore the situation, we need to know about core personality characteristics and situational characteristics, and the interaction between them both. Taking account of situations makes the process of attributing cause to effect in social situations much more difficult, and this is what attribution theory is all about. It is how we decide whether a person's behaviour can be attributed to an internal, core personality or dispositional characteristic ('he's looking over here because he likes me!'), or a situational characteristic ('oh, oops, he's looking over here because his friend is behind me').

The power of the situation

Kurt Lewin started out his scientific career as a physicist, but was driven to understand the mechanics of the social mind through his experiences of the Holocaust in World War II. He believed that just like objects in the physical universe, people's behaviour is influenced not only by their own intentions but also by a 'field of forces' in the (social) world around them. He believed that just as physicists can predict the speed and movement of an object moving through a medium, so too could psychologists predict the actions of people if they know the properties of the social medium in which they travelled. So, gravity, viscosity etc. become elements of the situation. This was a critical insight that shaped the next fifty years of research into the social mind: that to understand people, we need to understand them *in situ*. In other words, any person's action must be determined not only by their internal characteristics (desires, hopes, drives, etc.) but also by the characteristics of the situation in which they find themselves.

The power of the situation—in some cases the overwhelming power—is demonstrated in Philip Zimbardo's (in)famous Stanford Prison Experiment. In this early study of social behaviour, a group of volunteers were randomly split into two groups: prison guards and inmates. Zimbardo provided a range of strong situational elements to enhance the power of the randomly assigned role. As soon as they were assigned roles, the simulation began—inmates were dragged to a police station, fingerprinted, and stripped. Both the prison guards and inmates were deindividualized by being given just uniforms and numbers respectively, and the guards wore sunglasses to prevent eye contact.

What ensued was an incredible demonstration of the power of the situation in determining behaviour. The guards became increasingly immersed in their role—becoming more and more aggressive towards the inmates, and subjecting them to humiliation and degradation. Eventually the simulation had to be stopped because of fears for the safety of the inmates. This study showed the awesome power of social roles and situations in changing people's behaviour (remember that the guards and inmates were totally randomly assigned, and all well-adjusted, typical US citizens before entering the simulation).

Throughout this book I'll show you many examples of how social roles, stereotypes, categories, crowds, and a whole host of other situational determinants can bring out the darkest side of human behaviour (from Nazi guards 'just following orders', to the recent Abu Ghraib prison atrocities in Iraq). For now, what's important is that these studies demonstrate that any person's behaviour cannot be explained by their personality, drives, or motivations *alone*. We have to take account of the situation as well.

Making attributions

So any person's behaviour can have a cause internal to that person (disposition, personality, mood) or a cause external to that person (situation, luck, the influence of other people). Attribution theory is about the process that enables people to get to one or other of these conclusions. A number of theories about how people make attributions have been proposed over the years, but the best known is Kelley's co-variation model.

The co-variation model provides a set of rules for how people arrive at internal and external attributions for observed behaviour. To do so, Kelley believed that people look for three types of information: *consensus*, *consistency*, and *distinctiveness* information. This information is then integrated to compute the most likely cause of the behaviour at hand.

Say for example you arrive on campus one day and your best friend shimmies up to you sporting a crazy red wig. Immediately and automatically your social mind is asking the question 'why'? According to the co-variation model you look for the three key types of information.

First, consensus—is it just your friend who's wearing a red wig (low consensus), or is it everyone around you (high consensus)? If it's just your friend this implies a dispositional cause (something unique to your friend—perhaps they love to stand out from the

16

crowd). In contrast, if everyone is wearing a red wig this implies a situational cause (perhaps it's red wig charity day).

Second, consistency—does your friend always wear a red wig (high consistency) or are they only doing it today (low consistency). If your friend always wears a red wig this again implies the reason they're wearing it is because they like to stand out—it's part of their personality. If they're only doing it today then again this implies a situational cause—it's red wig day.

Third, distinctiveness—does your friend wear the red wig in other situations (low distinctiveness), or is it only on campus (high distinctiveness)? If it's in other situations as well, then again this implies a dispositional cause (it doesn't matter what the situation is, they want to express their personality by wearing wacky wigs). If however they don't wear red wigs in other situations, but just on campus, this implies a situational cause—again, red wig day.

According to the model people assess these three types of information, then go through a computation process to weigh up and combine the high versus low assessment for each. For instance, it may be that not all the types of information will be in alignment. Perhaps everybody on campus is wearing a red wig (high consensus, so implying a situational cause—red wig day), but also your friend *always* wears a wig anyway, and in different situations (high consistency and low distinctiveness, so implying a dispositional cause—their wacky personality). The model would predict that the perceiver then has to weigh up the conflicting consensus versus consistency and distinctiveness information and arrive at an overall judgement in which they decide to discount one of the pieces of information. In this case it is the consensus information that may be discounted or weighed less heavily into the eventual attribution, i.e. that your friend does still have a wacky personality and a desire to stand out, even though on this particular (red wig) day everyone else is wearing the red wig too.

While a fair amount of empirical evidence has accrued that people use these three types of information to draw conclusions about the causes of behaviour, it soon became apparent that formal models of attribution, like the co-variation model, were inherently limited. This was because in many cases people seemed to bypass the complex computations specified by these models, yet still make an attribution. Yes, studies showed that when people were given consensus, consistency, and distinctiveness information they were able to come to conclusions about the causes of people's behaviour as predicted by the co-variation model. However, miss out some of this information, or vary the conditions under which the judgement is required (e.g. time pressure, motivation), and the model breaks down. Instead, people appeared to make attributions using a whole different process. This other process was revealed in studies that found 'errors' when people were asked to make attributions under non-optimal or non-idealized conditions.

Attributional bias

I began this chapter suggesting that we are logical and rational in thinking about our social worlds: we act like naïve scientists in an attempt to construct a meaningful, predictive model of how other people behave. Well, that's true to an extent, but this desire for meaning and stability is not the only drive that determines how we think about others.

As research progressed on attribution theory it became apparent that much of the time we simply don't think like naïve scientists. We just don't go around 'testing hypotheses' about other people and their behaviour. We certainly don't do complex statistical computations in our heads every time we have a social interaction. Rather, we seem often to rely on things like 'gut feeling' and 'instinct' to form impressions of others—seemingly intangible thought processes that in fact can be isolated, defined, categorized, and predicted. This quicker, easier way of thinking was revealed in studies of *attributional bias*.

The first bias that people were found to display was named the *fundamental attribution bias* (FA bias) because people do it so often. It describes the tendency people have, all other things being equal, to make a dispositional (internal) attribution rather than a situational (external) attribution. Imagine you walk out of the nightclub one night and see two guys you don't know having a fight. What's your first thought? Probably not that they're both really nice people and simply acting out of character. If you met them in the pub the following week, your first impressions of them would probably stick—no matter how nice they seem, you saw them in a fight last week so that's going to colour your view of them now. In other words, your first thought is that the behaviour is indicative of a stable personality characteristic—a dispositional attribution.

Early evidence for this bias came from a study by Jones and Harris in 1967. They carried out a study during the Cold War in which they asked participants to read an essay that was pro-Fidel Castro as Cuban leader (this was around the time of the Cuban Missile Crisis). Participants were then asked to infer the attitudes of the writer. However, they were asked to do this after either being told that the author had freely chosen the topic of their essay *or* that their topic (pro-Castro) had been determined simply by the toss of a coin. Quite sensibly, people who were told that the writers chose to write a pro-Castro essay inferred that the writers indeed held attitudes that were pro-Castro. However, they *also* inferred that the writer was pro-Castro when they were told the topic was determined by the toss of a coin. In other words, even if they were told the writer was given *no choice* about the topic of the essay, they still made a dispositional attribution on the basis of the observed behaviour. This was all the more striking because at this point in history, in the US, there was widespread concern about Cuba and Castro's regime (i.e. the logical prediction would be that very few people would be pro-Castro).

The FA bias demonstrates that people do not always engage in complex statistical computations in their heads when trying to make attributions—instead they use some other source of information to make the decision. Research on a second bias, *the actor–observer bias*, demonstrates what this is. In 1973 Storms carried out a study similar to Jones and Harris and found that while people tended to make the FA bias when making attributions about others, when they were asked to make the same assessment about themselves they tended to make situational attributions. In other words, the FA bias was reversed.

The explanation for this is perceptual salience. Specifically, our attention is grabbed by whatever is most noticeable in the scene before us, and that is where we attribute causality. So, according to this explanation we make the FA error because the person in front of us is usually the most attention-grabbing thing in the scene—they are moving, talking, walking about. The situation is in the background, so we are much less likely to make a situational attribution, and more likely to make a dispositional one. On the other hand, when making attributions about our own behaviours we can't see ourselves in the scene. We're looking out on to the situation—so the situation becomes most attention grabbing for us.

Further support for the perceptual salience explanation is that it can be reversed simply by using a *mirror*. Research has shown that if you put a mirror in front of the participant when they are asked to make an attribution about their own behaviour then the effect is reversed: they are now likely to make the FA error about themselves (i.e. make a dispositional attribution). This is entirely in line with the perceptual salience explanation—in a mirror the attentional spotlight is again on us, making a dispositional attribution more likely.

Think about your everyday life, and you will notice that we do this all the time. If you meet someone who is rude and 'stand-offish' you probably come away thinking they're not a nice person (a dispositional attribution). However, if you meet someone and they catch you at a bad time, you don't suddenly change your idea of yourself and think you're horrible—you know you're in a bad mood because the dishwasher exploded at home this morning. In other words, you know about the situational factors that can account for your own behaviour, but you can't see how the same sort of situational factors affect others.

Using what is most perceptually salient to us to make attributions is a cognitive bias, but there are also biases that result from *motivations*. We are not just passive observers of the world around us—our hopes, needs, and desires also predict how we explain the behaviour of others, and ourselves, and often in a biased way. The *self-serving attribution bias* describes how sometimes attributions are made in ways that have nothing to do with computation, and nothing to do with perceptual salience—sometimes we simply make them in a way that will make us feel good.

Let's say you do particularly well in your social psychology exam. You probably will feel pretty good and pat yourself on the back for being clever and working hard—all dispositional attributions. You probably won't attribute it all to an external factor, i.e. luck. In contrast, if you do badly you'll feel much better if you put this down to bad luck with the choice of questions, or to the fact that you had a bad lecturer, instead of thinking you're just not that clever. Attributing success to internal causes, and failure to external causes, is one of the ways we regulate self-esteem and our view of our own self-worth.

These attributional biases and errors reveal that people don't always act like naïve scientists in their quest to create a stable, predictive model of the world around them. The drive that Heider identified tells us what guides the social mind in its exploration of the world—but the mechanics of how it does this can vary. People don't only logically and rationally process information. Instead they take shortcuts like perceptual salience, or motivations colour and filter our view of the world. These shortcuts have been discovered in areas of thinking that extend well beyond attributional judgements, and it is this research that shaped an entirely different view of social cognition.

The cognitive miser

The discovery of attributional errors and bias revealed a second side to the social mind. This second side was not rational, logical, careful, and systematic, but instead took an easier road to social judgement, relying on cues such as perceptual salience. But if people are not (always) naïve scientists, what are they? In their seminal thesis *Social Cognition*, Fiske and Taylor proposed we are something else entirely—we're *cognitive misers*.

Cognitive misers are the opposite of naïve scientists; they're not systematic and logical. They don't put lots of effort into thinking and analysing the world around them. Instead they rely on timesaving mental shortcuts known as heuristics. The cognitive miser is not so concerned with the world making sense; they're just concerned with expending cognitive resources as efficiently as possible. The cognitive miser is essentially a mental accountant who knows we only have so much we can think about at any one time—so they develop shortcuts known as heuristics to try to approximate the outcomes reached by the naïve scientist (in a quicker and less effortful way).

Heuristics are therefore timesaving mental shortcuts that allow us to make judgements without having to spend a great deal of time analysing or processing information. For instance, a strategy of relying on perceptual salience to make an attribution is a much easier and quicker way of making an attribution than laboriously looking for consensus, consistency, and distinctiveness information (and then computing, analysing, and combining this information to make a judgement). Such shortcuts are quick and easy, but this efficiency comes at a cost. While heuristics are generally accurate

22

(otherwise we wouldn't use them), they are much less accurate than the systematic thinking strategies used by the naïve scientist, and can therefore lead to a number of errors and bias such as those observed in the attribution field.

Perhaps the most researched heuristic is the *availability heuristic*. This is the heuristic that can explain the impact of perceptual salience on attributional judgements. In essence, people's judgements are steered, anchored, and sometimes hijacked by what is most attention grabbing in the context at hand, or what most readily comes to mind.

Imagine, for instance, you're about to get on a plane to fly off on your summer holiday. As you're about to board, on the TV screens in the departure lounge there's breaking news of a plane that has crashed somewhere in North America. Now, the fact that this crash is on the news right now has no substantive impact whatsoever on the probability that your plane will crash (flying will still be statistically safer than almost any other form of travel, this latest crash won't change that). However, despite knowing this logically, you probably wouldn't be able to help but feel a little more nervous than usual as you board the plane. This is the availability heuristic in operation. You may realize it's not logical, but just the ease with which you can recall the news item can have a profound impact on your 'gut feeling' about travelling.

One can think back to the weeks following the 9/11 Al Qaeda attacks in New York in 2001—there was an almost 20 per cent reduction in air travel. This was a cultural event that *seemed* to make air travel much more dangerous than it was because it was so salient in people's minds (statistically the 9/11 attacks had a negligible impact on the actual safety of air travel compared to other forms of travel).

The availability heuristic is behind a range of other phenomena in judgement and decision-making, perhaps most notably the *false consensus effect*. Over one hundred studies have shown that people have a general tendency to believe that most other people agree with them on whatever issue is at hand. Of course, our own opinions are the most available to us, especially when they are strongly held (i.e. we recall them a lot) and we have no clear indication of the views of others (e.g. they're not physically present, or are distributed over a large network).

Social priming

The heuristics discussed in this chapter demonstrate how the cognitive miser uses shortcuts in everyday thinking. What's important for our understanding of the social mind is how shortcuts are also used in forming impressions of others. One way in which the availability heuristic can affect the impressions we form of other people is through priming effects. Solomon Asch was a pioneering social psychologist who we'll come across a lot in this book. He demonstrated how people can be incredibly biased in the information they remember about someone on a first meeting. In his 1946 experiment he gave two groups of participants a list of adjectives describing someone. The first group received the following attributes, presented in precisely this order: intelligent, industrious, impulsive, critical, stubborn, envious.

They were then asked to say what they thought this person was like. On the whole, participants thought this person would be a nice person to meet and evaluated them positivity. In contrast, Asch gave a second group of participants precisely the same list of adjectives but this time in the opposite order: envious, stubborn, critical, impulsive, industrious, intelligent.

When asked to form an impression, this time the group gave a much less positive evaluation. This study demonstrates the power of the availability heuristic. People remember the most available information, and it has been shown that people particularly remember the first few pieces of information they receive when meeting someone for the first time.

This social priming is pervasive in everyday cognition. It's a good example of how the social mind can be a cognitive miser and a naïve scientist at the same time. On the one hand, it is a time-saving mental shortcut that reduces the amount of processing required. On the other hand, it helps us construct predictive mental models from first impressions. Remember how Heider thought we have a basic desire for consistency and predictability? Social priming can be seen as a manifestation of this. Our desire to create structure and meaning is so pervasive we start to do it right from when we begin receiving information. What happens is that the initially received information creates a structure that then filters the remaining information—leading to something called a confirmation bias. So, for instance, if you form an impression of someone as 'industrious' and then they display stubborn behaviour, you may be more likely to interpret this as 'steadfast and determined'. If, in contrast, your first impression is of them as 'envious', then stubborn behaviour is more likely to be interpreted as 'close-minded' and 'rigid'. This research suggests that first impressions really do count!

This framing effect is also evident in how people describe big issues. Think about conflicts around the world, and the way in which opposing groups and governments talk about them—do they refer to 'freedom fighters' or 'terrorists', 'occupiers' or 'peacekeepers'? How something is labelled can fundamentally change the way subsequent information is interpreted, and this can be used to great effect in the media, law and politics. Framing is critical to how we process information; to how we form attitudes and impressions.

John Bargh demonstrated how even seemingly irrelevant information can create such a frame. In his 1996 'language study' he asked participants to first unscramble words to form a series of sentences. Unbeknown to the participants, this task was actually designed to create a frame. Half the participants unscrambled words to form sentences that referred to polite behaviour, and half unscrambled sentences that ended up referring to rude behaviour. After this, participants thought the experiment was over and went off to a second experiment (a study in which they would converse with another participant). The dependent measure was how often the participant would interrupt the experimenter conversing with the other participant. Participants who had received the rude prime interrupted the experimenter much more than the participants who had received the politeness prime. This shows that (a) frames can affect not only our impression of others but also our behaviour, and (b) frames can affect actions that are unrelated to the context in which they were formed.

Our compulsion to automatically create meaning in social situations is not just done 'on line', i.e. shaped by the early pieces of information we receive about someone. We carry around with us a huge number of these filters and frames based upon previous experience, and they start shaping the information we process about people as soon as (and indeed before) we even meet them. These frames are called schemas, scripts, and stereotypes.

Scripts, schemas and stereotypes

Scripts and schemas are shortcuts for understanding the world. They adhere to the same basic principles as outlined for framing effects, but they are more detailed and complex, stored in memory, and activated when we encounter specific situations in our everyday life that trigger them. They are mini mental models of how our social universe works.

Take going to the cinema. When you arrive your script kicks in: you know you need to go to the ticket booth, then the confectionary counter, then head to the right screen, and then stop talking once the lights go down. You know you don't push to the front of the queue at the ticker counter, sit in seats other than those indicated on your ticket, you don't stand up or talk loudly once the film has started or begin singing at the top of your voice just because you're happy! There's a script for what behaviours are (a) necessary and (b) acceptable in this social context.

Think of all the other scripts that kick in during everyday life. Driving, going to the supermarket, cooking a meal from a well-memorized recipe. We know that in a fast food restaurant we go up to counter, in a posh restaurant we wait to be served. Next time you see a traffic jam part like waves to let an ambulance through, think about what is happening—everyone in every car knows precisely what they need to do in that situation. It is a socially shared script that is activated in response to a specific environmental cue (the ambulance siren).

Scripts are formed through experience—just like learning to ride a bicycle. Once a script has been formed and activated it can influence a whole range of expectations, intentions, interpretations, and behaviours. In many ways scripts operate like the availability heuristic coming to mind when the situation fits. While incredibly useful and functional in everyday life, these cognitive shortcuts have a use that can have a negative impact on people's lives, and this is when they apply to groups of people.

Schemas are what are brought to mind as a result of basic categorization processes. For instance, think of an item of 'fruit'. Got it? I bet you thought of an *apple* or an *orange*—these are the most frequently recalled items when people think of the category 'fruit'. Now think of a mechanic. I bet you thought of a man. Being a male is the occupational schema of the category mechanic.

Schemas about groups of people are stereotypes. They fit the description of heuristics perfectly. They are rules of thumb— shortcuts that enable us to make assumptions about people, and predict their behaviour, without having to engage in effortful and time-consuming mental processes. These shortcuts and

27

assumptions can be incredibly useful. In a medical emergency expecting a doctor (versus a plumber) to have the knowledge needed to save someone's life is critical. On the other hand, when you've got a leak at home you know a plumber can help (but not a dentist), and so on.

These expectations about people help us structure and give meaning to our worlds, while also being incredibly efficient ways of forming first impressions about people. Stereotypes mean that we don't have to be naïve scientists to create our mental model of the world, and from a purely functional view this makes sense. In a medical emergency we simply don't have the time to spend several minutes questioning a doctor to ascertain, logically and rationally, from the information provided, whether he has the requisite medical knowledge.

The trouble with stereotypes is that, like all the framing effects described so far, they significantly bias the interpretation of new information. This is particularly problematic when they are based upon erroneous or unfairly negative information in the first place. The framing and filtering effect of stereotypes have been demonstrated in numerous studies. In one study participants were played a videotape of a woman having a birthday dinner. Participants told she was *either* a waitress *or* a librarian (creating the stereotypic frame). If told the former, participants showed better recall for the woman drinking beer; if told the latter, they showed better recall for the women wearing glasses.

This confirmation bias has been shown to affect really important social decision-making. For instance, studies have shown mock juries are more likely to perceive an ethnic minority defendant as guilty (versus a white defendant) on the basis of *exactly* the same case evidence—but only if the name (which is a clear label for ethnicity) is presented before the information. So doing creates the frame that changes the interpretation of the subsequently presented information. This can also be a real problem for a society striving to create equality of opportunity and tolerance for all. For instance, if a women cannot get a job in a 'male' field like engineering or science *because* she is a women (i.e. the counter-stereotypic gender for that occupation), then this is an example of a stereotype propagating inequality and bias.

Stereotypes are also hard to change because they are maintained through language. The *linguistic intergroup bias* describes how language can transmit and maintain these associations. Specifically, people encode, represent, and use positive behaviours about their own group, and negative behaviours about other groups, in an *abstract* way; but positive behaviours about other groups, and negative behaviours about their own group, in a *concrete* way. Importantly, abstract language implies that the focal topic is an enduring, stable characteristic while concrete language implies a one-off, isolated example. In this way the association of one's own group with positive feelings and other groups with negative feelings can become self-perpetuating. We'll discuss how negative stereotypes are formed, and how their use can lead to prejudice, intolerance, and inequality, in detail in Chapter 5.

The motivated tactician

In this chapter we've seen how people can be logical and systematic in their processing of information about people, or they can be quick and efficient—but with the increased risk of errors. Which is correct? Studies have shown that both apply, and that's precisely right: we are both naïve scientists and cognitive misers—but which we are depends upon the situation. The best way to think about how both models apply is to separate the components of Heider's original notion of the naïve scientist into (a) underlying drive and (b) process. The fundamental desire driving the social mind is to create a predictive model of our social universe, but this can be achieved through one of two processes. Either it can be achieved through the reasoned, systematic, and logical mechanics of thinking specified by the naïve scientist *or* it can be achieved through the more efficient, but error prone, heuristics used by the cognitive miser. In other words, we can create a predictive model of our social universe using either mode of thinking, depending upon what works for the current situation.

Characteristics of the situation appear to predict when either processing route is engaged. People rely on stereotypes when they have little other information to go on, or when they are in a rush or busy (i.e. they have low motivation to engage more effortful but accurate systematic processing). In contrast, when people are motivated to be accurate, or if information is available that shows the person clashes with their stereotypic expectations, then people are more likely to 'snap out' of stereotypes and form an impression. The social mind therefore has two modes of thinking available to it: one slow, effortful and accurate versus one quick, easy, but sometimes inaccurate. These two ways of forming impressions are summed up by the *continuum model* of impression formation.

According to the continuum model the default mode of processing is heuristic. So when we first encounter someone new we try to fit them into a social category: are they male or female, young or old, Christian or Muslim, and so on. For the most fundamental categories (gender, age, and race) this happens within the first few milliseconds. If the person fits the category then the stereotype is applied and filters all subsequent information.

However, sometimes both internal drives and situational factors can lead perceivers to move away from the heuristic end of the continuum towards the systematic thinking end. For instance, if the stranger is someone interviewing you, then you're likely to automatically shift to the systematic processing (high attention) end of the continuum. Alternatively, if the person does not fit an existing category, or conflicts with expectations (e.g. a female mechanic, Figure 1) then existing stereotypes are of no use and so abandoned as a means of impression formation. Now the naïve

1. **A female mechanic. People who disconfirm stereotypes can encourage a revision of existing beliefs about social roles.**

scientist kicks in, increasing cognitive resource allocation in an attempt to make sense of the person at hand. Essentially, this is the naïve scientist attempting to revise their mental model of the world around them, to ensure they can maintain a high level of predictability. If they just ignored exceptions to the rule like this then eventually the system would break down.

In this way the cognitive miser and the naïve scientist work in perfect harmony with each other. The cognitive miser monitors the world around them, applying the rules of their mental model (the scripts, schemas and stereotypes). When, however, someone is encountered who does not confirm to the rules, who does not fit into the system, this indicates revisions to the system are needed. That's where the naïve scientist steps in to provide a detailed, systematic analysis of the person at hand, and to revise the mental model. The revised model is then applied to future interactions and the whole process begins again. In this way, some social psychologists have suggested we are, in fact, *motivated tacticians*, adopting the processing strategy that best helps us make sense of the world. This may also be the way that, over time, stereotypes change. As increasingly we are exposed to people in counter-stereotypic roles (such as female mechanics), so our stereotypes of what is the norm for different occupations can be revised.

So that's the social mind, the nuts and bolts of thinking about people. These mechanics will guide what we encounter in the rest of this book. As we progress keep in mind these basic principles. People are seeking to make sense of the world around them, to build a model of their social universe that enables them to predict how others will behave, and enables them to realize and reach their goals and aspirations.

Chapter 3
Attitudes and influence

We now know the basic workings of the social mind, and the mechanisms that help us create a predictive model of our social universe—but what about the content? Our mental models are made up of *attitudes*. Attitudes are a set of beliefs about an object, person, or issue. They can be simple and clear, or complex and multifaceted. They are the basic building blocks of our mental models—they are the specific content that helps us predict why the world is the way it is, and whether we think it should be different. They inform and guide our ideals and aspirations, values, and ideology.

If the sub-field of social cognition describes the physics of how we construct a mental model of our social universe, attitudes are what determine the characteristics of that model. Attitudes predict our behaviour, and are therefore integral to who we are, what we do, and why we do it. In this chapter I'll discuss how attitudes form, change, and predict behaviour. I'll discuss how they are inherently social; defined and refined in response to people in the world around us.

Attitude formation

In 1968 Robert Zajonc (pronounced 'science') published a paper that was to revolutionize thinking about attitude formation. In his

Of these two objects below, which one do you like better?
Please indicate your response by typing the 'left' or 'right' key.

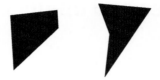

2. Zajonc's mere exposure symbols.

study participants were exposed to ten Chinese-like characters for two seconds each (Figure 2). Importantly, the characters were completely made up, and participants could never have seen them anywhere before. Each of the characters was presented for a different amount of time (five times, ten times, fifteen times, etc.). After this the participants were presented with the characters again and asked to guess whether each was a word that indicated something positive or negative. What Zajonc found was that people showed a clear tendency to like the characters that had been presented for longer durations.

There have been hundreds of replications of this 'mere exposure' effect—with a whole variety of different stimuli—from people to food to statements referring to complex social issues. The accumulated evidence leaves the veracity of the effect in little doubt: the more we see something, the more we like it.

Mere exposure represents the most basic mechanism of attitude formation: we like things we are familiar with. This makes perfect sense when we consider the basic needs that drive the social mind covered in Chapter 2. The social mind needs to construct a meaningful mental model of the world, one that enables us to predict the behaviour of others, and how social contexts work. What is familiar is predictable—so it makes sense that we would have evolved to feel good when we see familiar things. Mere exposure represents the most basic manifestation of the social mind building a predictive model of our social universe.

The effect can even explain curiosities such as how we never like photographs of ourselves, while our friends do and can't see why we don't. The reason is that we are very unfamiliar with seeing ourselves from a photographer's (external) perspective. The perspective we are much more familiar with is the mirror image of ourselves. This is because we see our mirror image all the time; and because no one is perfectly symmetrical our mirror image appears just slightly different from the view other people have of us.

While the more we see something the more we like it, this basic effect is qualified by the associated feelings that frame our experiences. Learning by association is another way that our social minds learn what to approach, and what to avoid, in the world around us. Learning by association is enabled by one of the oldest systems in the human brain—one that we even share with animals. We're attuned to detect co-variation in our environments: when two things occur at the same time, enough times, we come to expect one to lead to the other. The famous example is Ivan Pavlov's experiment where he paired a bell with the delivery of food to a dog. He found that after a while the bell on it's own was enough to elicit salivating in the dog. This is because the dog had learned that food followed the bell. Well, you can get the same learning by association in humans, and with social stimuli too.

Carolyn and Arthur Staats carried out an experiment in which participants were exposed to the words 'Dutch' or 'Swedish' simultaneously accompanied by words with positive or negative connotations. Participants were subsequently asked to indicate their feelings to a whole range of nationalities, including those associated with positive or negative words in the learning phase. Sure enough, when Dutch was paired with positive, participants subsequently felt more positive towards the word 'Dutch', and when 'Swedish' was paired with negative participants subsequently felt more negative towards the word 'Swedish'. When the experimenters reversed the pairings in the learning phase (Dutch–Negative and Swedish–Positive), how participants subsequently felt towards the nationality labels followed suit.

Notably, the effect is stronger when the positive or negative words are paired with nonsense words, suggesting that associative learning may be a more important determinant of attitudes when people have little prior knowledge of the issue, object, or person at hand. This makes sense: learning by association is how we build our mental model of the world. Once established, they can be hard to change (as we have seen with scripts, schemas and framing in Chapter 2). A mental model of how the world works is only useful if it doesn't change at the drop of a hat.

As well as the basic learning mechanism described by mere exposure and learning by association, people can form and express attitudes in a conscious attempt to exert control over their social universe. The functional theory to attitude formation argues that we actively adopt attitudes that support, develop, and define important goals that we hold. Attitudes like this can also be value-expressive. Someone who loves animals may develop strong support for the NSPCA. Conversely, the Greenpeace or LGBT rights campaigner will likely have developed attitudes earlier on that are consistent with the core beliefs that encourage their roles.

Alternatively, people can hold attitudes to fit in with groups, to build bonds and consensus, or to appease and please significant others. This is the utilitarian function—the idea that we express (and hold) attitudes to make it easier for us to form relationships. So some people might hold the same attitude as their friends to fit in. If all your friends like a particular pop star and you don't, it might make it harder to find common ground, share in conversation, and engage in shared activities. You might have a friend who gets a boyfriend who really likes football and cars, then you find they've suddenly developed an interest in football and cars too. Your parents might both be teachers and would like nothing more than for you to follow in their footsteps, so you find yourself being drawn to a career in teaching. Attitudes like this help us fulfil our goals—they are a means to an end. They might not reflect our true or privately held attitudes, but that doesn't make them any less real, or less predictive of behaviour. We'll look at conformity and social influence, and the distinction between public and private attitudes, in more depth a little later on in this chapter.

As well as exerting control over our environment, attitudes also help us to build knowledge. This knowledge function enables us to predict the world, and fulfil this basic need of the social mind. For instance, if someone hates foreign food, this might lead him or her to construct an attitude that they don't like travelling abroad (or even that they don't like foreigners, and adopt anti-immigration views, and vice versa).

Finally, attitudes can also have an ego-defensive function—for instance, someone might be racist or blame immigrants for taking all the work available as a way of defending themselves against the prospect of negative self-esteem brought on by the knowledge that one is unemployed. Remember self-serving attributions covered in Chapter 2? These can drive the formation of ego-defensive attitudes. So, forming an attitude that one's teacher is a bad teacher is a way of externally attributing failure, and so protecting self-esteem.

When attitudes predict behaviour

The study of attitudes is interesting because it shows how we create a coherent model of our social universe. However, social psychologists don't only want to understand how people represent their social universe, they also want this knowledge to have practical use—and in particular to be able to predict how people will behave. If attitudes don't predict behaviour they are of little practical use in terms of things like education and social policy. Worryingly, early research suggested this was precisely the case!

In 1934 a psychologist called Richard LaPierre drove around the US with a Chinese couple, seeing how many hotels and restaurants would be happy to serve them. At this time in the US there was a lot of prejudice towards East Asians, so this was a study that tackled an important social issue. The idea was to see whether behaviour—in this case willingness to serve the Chinese couple, would be predicted by attitudes (the attitudes were measured later on via a telephone survey). What LaPierre found was that, despite the apparent widespread prejudice, just one out of 250 restaurants refused to serve the couple. However, a little later on, when he contacted the restaurants by *telephone* and tried to make a booking for another Chinese couple, he found a dramatically different pattern—90 per cent said they would refuse to serve them.

This was a shocking and quite disturbing result for a discipline attempting to establish itself as a useful social science. It suggested there was no point in studying attitudes at all because, quite simply, they didn't predict people's behaviour. Well, it turned out to be not quite as bad as all that. What emerged was that people's attitudes only predict behaviour *under certain circumstances*.

Actually, this makes a lot of sense. People are not one-dimensional, and as we saw in Chapter 2 behaviour is not always predicted by personality. We have to take the situation into account as well (even the biggest extrovert can show restraint at a funeral). So too it is with attitudes. They're an excellent basis for predicting behaviour, but we have to keep other factors in mind as well. For instance, to predict behaviour attitudes must be measured at the same level of specificity.

Take LaPierre's study: he contacted the restaurant owners to ask if they would serve Chinese people in *general*, but when he actually visited he asked whether they would serve a *specific* Chinese couple. Attitudes about general groups of people can be very different from attitudes towards individuals who happen to be members of that group. Another factor is social desirability. As we'll see later in this chapter, people are highly concerned with how they look in front of other people, and if there is a social norm of politeness (for example) this may override any privately held attitudes. So, you may really not like your girlfriend or boyfriend's friends—but bite your tongue when you're all together to preserve the peace!

Attitudes also change over time. LaPierre's attitude assessment occurred many months after the behaviour was assessed. As discussed, the social mind is constantly on the look out for exceptions to the rule, be they people, events, or things that make our mental models less efficient at predicting how others will behave. The social mind is a dynamic system, and one that is constantly growing, revising, and changing. Our attitudes change over time (just think about your opinions on a range of issues a few years ago—political, cultural, social—are they all the same or have some dramatically changed?). The longer the time period between assessing an attitude and measuring behaviour, the less in line they're likely to be.

LaPierre's research spawned a great deal of subsequent work on the attitude–behaviour relationship, and gave rise to one of the most influential theories in social psychology: the *theory of planned behaviour*. According to Icek Ajzen, attitudes are one of three key predictors of behaviour, along with subjective norms and perceived control. Subjective norms are what significant others think you *should* do—family, teachers, boss, etc. So if giving up smoking is the behaviour, then a smoker's girlfriend wanting them to give up is a subjective norm. Perceived control is whether you can actually perform the behaviour, e.g. whether a smoker actually believes he can give up smoking. These three factors combine to predict behavioural intention, in turn predicting behaviour.

Research has embellished this core model, and other factors are important in different situations. For instance, past behaviour (e.g. habits) can make it more or less likely that a behaviour will be carried out (depending on whether they are in line with the behavioural intention). Furthermore, the link between intentions and behaviour is strengthened by encouraging people to make specific plans called 'implementation intentions'. Implementation intentions take the form: 'I intend to do [y] when situation [x] arises', so the intention is linked to a specific behaviour. Then, when the relevant situation arises, it triggers the if–then plan. Studies have confirmed the benefits of implementation intentions for goal achievement in a range of domains including health (breast self-examination) and academic performance (report writing).

When behaviour predicts attitudes

So far we've assumed that attitudes come before behaviour in the run of things. However, sometimes attitudes can be formed, or change, *after* the behaviour is performed. This is through a 'meta-cognitive' process of self-perception. Meta-cognition refers to people thinking about thinking. It is like stepping back and considering 'why did I think/say/do that?'

According to Daryl Bem's *self-perception theory* this is one of the ways in which we form attitudes—we take a step back, look at our own past behaviour, and then infer what our attitude must be. It is a type of attribution (see Chapter 2), where we attribute causality to our own behaviours, determining whether they are driven by internal dispositional characteristics (i.e. our attitudes) or by situational constraints (e.g. 'just going along with the crowd').

For instance, if someone asks you if you're environmentally friendly you might think, 'well, I recycle at home and at school so yes I must be'. Research has found just this: ask people questions that highlight their pro-environmental behaviour (e.g. recycling) versus anti-environmental behaviour (e.g. how much lighting, heating they use) and they subsequently report themselves as a 'greener' person. However, this only happens when people don't have a strong attitude already formed on the subject at hand. For instance, a Greenpeace campaigner will likely report that they are pro-environmental however you frame the question to them.

You can even get these self-perception effects from facial feedback. Research has shown that simply being asked to place a pen in one's teeth (making one's face form a smile) as opposed to one's lips (making one's face form a frown) leads people to like cartoons more. Again, this can be seen as an illustration of attribution theory (see Chapter 2). People *mis*-attribute the cause of their smiling or frowning to the cartoon in front of them—the most salient situational cause available to them.

Another way in which behaviour can change attitudes is through something called *cognitive dissonance*. Cognitive dissonance theory was developed by Leon Festinger in 1957. It is based upon the Freudian idea that people experience psychological discomfort whenever they reflect on behaviours (they have performed) that are *counter* to the attitudes they hold. The theory predicts that this 'dissonance' between attitudes held and behaviours expressed will change attitudes to bring them in line with their behaviour. This is because you can't undo the behaviour (it's done, it's in the past), and so changing your attitude is the only way you can resolve the uncomfortable 'dissonance' between your attitudes and the behaviour you performed. This is, once again, the social mind seeking stability, structure, and meaning. If we don't act in line with our own attitudes, then how can our mental model of the world predict anything?

Festinger and James Carlsmith provided a compelling demonstration of cognitive dissonance in 1959. They asked participants to carry out a boring task (repeatedly turning forty-eight wooden pegs on a board for an hour). After this, half the participants were asked to lie to the next participant—to tell them that it was a fun and enjoyable task (prior testing had confirmed that participants really did find the peg task boring). After the experiment participants were contacted and asked if they really did enjoy the task. Festinger and Carlsmith found that in the baseline condition participants unsurprisingly reported that they didn't enjoy it. However, participants who had been told to lie to the next participant reported actually enjoying the task. In other words, their attitude towards the task had apparently changed because they had been asked to lie.

Interestingly, the effect disappears when, before lying, participants are given a reward (in this case $20). Festinger and Carlsmith argue that this is because people then have a justification for why they lied. Without a reward however (or when the reward is too small), the memory of what they did causes the unpleasant psychological feeling of cognitive dissonance. Because the event that caused the dissonance occurred in the past, the event itself cannot be changed, so the only way to remove this uncomfortable feeling is to change the only thing that can be changed—one's current attitude.

Attitude change through cognitive dissonance is similar to the process described by *self-perception theory*, but it has one crucial difference—it operates when initially a strong (as opposed to weak) attitude is held. The two theories operate in slightly different ways to serve the social mind's underlying motivation to make sense of the world. Self-perception theory applies when people are unsure of their attitude on a particular topic (i.e. they have a weak attitude). As such they infer their attitude from their behaviour as a way of reducing uncertainty; it is a way of *constructing* their mental model of the world around them. Cognitive dissonance applied when people already have a strong attitude about a particular topic, but they act in a way that is counter to this attitude. Here, attitude change occurs as a way of *modifying* their mental model of the world around them. This is important so the model can maintain its predictive utility. Attitudes are not much use if they don't predict behaviour, and attitude change through cognitive dissonance is a way of maintaining this critical function.

Persuasion

So far we've looked at how attitudes form or change due to either internal desires, or people reacting to events in their environment. Sometimes, however, other people are involved. In other words, someone is trying to persuade us to change our attitude.

In contrast to the attitude change we've just discussed, persuasion is attitude change as the result of intended *external* influence. While cognitive dissonance and self-perception are both instances of attitude change as a result of internal self-reflection, persuasion is attitude change after being exposed to someone else trying to change our attitude. One of the best-known models of persuasion is the *elaboration-likelihood model* (ELM) proposed by Richard Petty and John Cacioppo in 1986. The ELM is a dual-process model just like Fiske and Neuberg's continuum model of impression formation that I discussed in Chapter 2. In other words, it is derived directly from the 'motivated tactician' view of the social mind, here applied to attitude change.

According to the model, persuasion can occur through two processing routes: a central route and a peripheral route. When the central route is taken then persuasive messages are processed in a systematic and analytic way (high 'elaboration'). This is the naïve scientist in action. Central route processing might occur when the issue at hand is really important to us. Here the information is scrutinized and we come to a logical and rational conclusion, very much like the processes outlined by Kelley's co-variation model of attribution. If, in contrast, the peripheral

43

route is taken then we act like cognitive misers. So rather than devoting mental energy to scrutinize arguments we are persuaded by quick and easy cues like how attractive the person trying to persuade us is. This is a heuristic way of thinking just like reliance on perceptual salience to make attributions (see Chapter 2).

Whether we take the central or peripheral route depends upon things like how much time and information we have available and how motivated we are. However, there are other peripheral cues like *humour* and *mood* that can determine which route is taken. For instance, evolutionary psychologists have speculated that a negative mood signals something wrong with the environment, so this triggers an increase in attentiveness (high elaboration) in order to identify any possible threats to survival. In contrast, happy people tend to use the peripheral route. This suggests that happy people are more susceptible to weak cues like attractiveness.

Another factor is issue involvement. When the outcome of argument has important consequences for the self the central route is taken. For instance, if your response may be scrutinized by others and lead to social approval/disapproval. Individual differences are also important. Someone with a high need for cognition (a preference to engage in effortful thought) will, if the information is available, be more likely to take the central route. Similarly, self-monitoring (the degree to which someone is concerned about the views of others) will gravitate people to processing via the central route.

Finally, factors like speed of speech are influential. For instance, if the person trying to persuade us is speaking rapidly this makes it difficult to process the content of what they are saying. This can then compel people to process the message using the peripheral route.

Importantly, whether the central or the peripheral route is taken does not determine whether the person will be persuaded. In other words, people are not just more persuaded when they use the central route rather than the peripheral route. Rather, whether someone is persuaded or not depends upon whether the central route or peripheral route *cues* are compelling.

So, rapid speech may make someone take the peripheral route (the information needed for systematic processing is simply not available)—but whether the person is persuasive or not depends upon what makes those peripheral cues compelling, factors like source attractiveness and credibility. However, attitudes formed via the peripheral route are weaker, less resistant to counter argument, and less predictive of behaviour than central route attitudes.

Social influence

An important observation about the research discussed so far is that, for the most part, it has focused on situational or internal drivers of attitude formation. Mere exposure and associative learning are situational drivers (the amount of exposure to the attitude object). Self-perception and cognitive dissonance are internal, meta-cognitive processes (thinking about one's behaviour, and whether it reflects one's attitude). Finally, persuasion is attitude change as a result of a persuasive message—someone trying to change our attitudes. The latter represents the most 'social' influence on attitudes; that is, attitude change that results from interacting (in a broad sense) with other people. In the remaining part of this chapter we are going to delve more deeply into this type of social influence.

Social norms

While persuasion involves someone trying to change our attitudes, sometimes attitudes can change simply because we are in the presence of others. Social psychology is all about groups, and some of the very earliest experiments looked at how other people affected our internally held attitudes. In fact, some would argue that Musaf Sherif's 1935 study on norm development sums up what social psychology is all about—the great impact that other people have on our attitudes, values, and behaviour.

In Sherif's study, participants were asked to sit in a dark room with a single dot of light projected in front of them. Sherif was making use of an established perceptual illusion—the 'autokinetic effect'. This effect describes the tendency of light to appear to move when there is no reference point (e.g. a dot of light in a dark room). The participants' task was to estimate how far the dot of light was oscillating back and forth. They repeated this judgement on a number of trials, over and over again.

When participants did this task on their own they all came up with slightly different estimates of how far the dot was moving in its oscillations (this is the nature of the illusion; in fact it is not moving at all). However, when they were asked to do the task with other people present, something extraordinary happened—their estimates began to converge. On successive trials the estimates participants made moved closer and closer to a common norm.

This was one of the first ever demonstrations of *social influence*, and when you think about it, it's really quite striking. We all like to think our attitudes are our own, and that they are unaffected by those around us (especially strangers). Here, however, is a clear demonstration that what participants thought were their own objective judgements were actually an emergent property of the social context. Participants were blissfully unaware of the influence the context exerted on what they believed were accurate judgements.

Sherif's classic study opened up a whole new area of social influence research, and profoundly illustrated the power of others to affect our attitudes. With persuasion we usually know someone is trying to change our minds (at least if we are paying attention, and processing the message via the central route). Here, participants had no idea about the effect other people were having on their judgements, and this is what makes social influence so important and powerful for understanding everyday social cognition.

Think about the last time you were debating something in a group and came around to the majority view being expressed by others in the room. Was it because everyone came to an agreement based upon the key facts and systematic processing of the information? Alternatively, was it because of social norm pressures, guiding you to think you were coming to a reasoned decision, when in fact there was unseen social influence exerting an effect?

Interestingly, the rate upon which people converge on a group norm increases the more uncertain people are about the task. This convergence can be seen as an illustration of the social mind attempting to build a mental model of its social environment. The participants in Sherif's experiment didn't have much information, so could not systematically and rationally process the relevant information. Instead they had to look for cues to make a quick, approximate judgement. In Chapter 2 we saw how people expect others to share their attitudes with the *false consensus effect*—here the process works the other way. Participants could not be sure of their judgement so they looked to the judgements of others as a guide.

But what about when we are not uncertain about the judgements we're giving? What about when we have a clear belief that we are correct, and everyone else is wrong? Is there still social influence when there is no uncertainty? The answer is yes, and to a surprising degree.

Conformity

In 1951 Solomon Asch carried out what was to become one of the defining experiments of social psychology. In his study

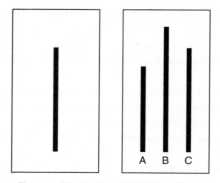

3. Comparison lines used in Asch's conformity study.

participants were asked to carry out a visual perception experiment, similar to the one carried out by Sherif's participants. Here, participants were required to compare a standard line with three comparison lines, and on successive trials call out which of the three comparison lines matched the standard line in terms of length. To test the effects of social influence, six other people were present. These people were not genuine participants like they were in Sherif's study, but in fact confederates of the experimenter. In other words, unbeknown to the single genuine participant, the six other participants were in league with the experimenter and were responding throughout to a pre-prepared script.

The experiment went as follows. On each trial the standard line was presented followed by the comparison lines (Figure 3). All of the participants, who were sitting around a table, called out their answer one by one. They called out A, B, or C depending upon which of the three lines they thought matched the standard line.

Five of the confederates called out the line before the participant. Where it got interesting was that after the first two trials, the confederates began to give what were clearly incorrect answers.

For instance, they would say, 'line B' when line B was clearly an inch or so longer than the standard line, and where line A was clearly the correct answer. Furthermore, it was not just one confederate giving the incorrect answer—they all began to.

A key difference between Asch's line estimation experiment and Sherif's light estimation experiment is that in Sherif's study there was no clear answer (in fact any movement of light they perceived was an illusion). In Asch's study the correct answer was obvious. This was confirmed when participants completed the study on their own—they all chose the correct comparison line 99 per cent of the time.

So what would you do in this situation? Do you believe your ears (the wildly incorrect answer being given by everyone else) or do you believe your own eyes? The results were astounding. What Asch found was that participants gave an incorrect response on 37 per cent of the trials. In other words, when the confederates gave what the participant knew was a clearly incorrect answer, participants ignored their own eyes and also gave this incorrect answer. In fact, 76 per cent of participants went along with the incorrect majority on at least one of the trials.

So why did people conform? There are two types of social influence. One is informational influence. This is what was operating in Sherif's light estimation experiment that I discussed earlier. Informational influence is using other people's attitudes as a rule of thumb when you're uncertain about what response to give. It is the social mind seeking to build a mental model of the situation.

That's not what was happening in Asch's study though—everyone got the judgement correct when they were on their own, so they clearly knew the right answer. Here a different type of influence was operating: normative influence. Normative influence is the desire to simply 'fit in'. When we stand out from the group, when we don't fit in, or when we are highlighted as being different, we find this aversive. In fact, research shows that it literally hurts. Brain-scanning studies have shown that the physical pain centre of the brain is activated when we are excluded from groups.

This makes a lot of sense from an evolutionary point of view. Groups were always adaptive for a social species like humans. In our ancestors' world to be included in the 'tribe' was to feel secure and safe from danger, but to be excluded meant a serious survival problem (we'll discuss the primitive, visceral impact of social exclusion in more depth in Chapter 6).

In subsequent studies, various factors that strengthen or weaken conformity were uncovered. For instance, the greater the number of people present, the stronger the normative influence. Research has shown that the percentage number of trials on which people conform increases up to about three people, then levels off at about 37 per cent. Variants of the original study have shown that when you maximize conditions that promote informational influence you get increased conformity (e.g. the standard line doesn't remain visible when the judgement is required, making the whole task more uncertain). Importantly, this shows that informational influence can operate when you make the task more uncertain, but the effect is independent from normative influence. In other words, it is not that as informational influence increases normative influence decreases. Uncertainty doesn't decrease the desire to fit in, if anything it makes it even more important.

The two types of influence can also be distinguished by the effect they have on private versus public attitudes. Remember that in Asch's experiment it was the publically expressed attitude that changed—participants didn't really change their beliefs about the length of the line, they just wanted to avoid being the odd one out. Normative influence (when things are certain and clear, but there is group pressure) changes public but not private attitudes—this is known as 'compliance'. Informational influence (when the task is difficult, there is little info, or the participant is uncertain) changes both public *and* private attitudes—this is known as 'conversion'.

Further variants of the Asch study revealed other interesting phenomena to do with conformity. Most notably, social support that breaks the consensus dramatically decreases conformity, even if it is just one of the confederates who agrees with the participant. This is the case even if the confederate does not agree with the participant (i.e. they are still giving an incorrect answer, it is just that they are also diverging from the majority). What is important here is the breaking of social consensus. However, if the defector then switches back to the majority, conformity returns to the pre-break level. Social support is a powerful tool for resisting conformity, but the minority consensus it builds is fragile (there is apparently a lot of truth to the old adage 'divide and rule').

Minority influence

From the research discussed so far you might think that majorities always get their way, but sometimes psychological processes can conspire to elicit powerful minority influence. Serge Moscovici carried out another visual perception experiment to investigate social influence, but this time with the minority as the influencer.

In his study, participants were shown a series of either green or blue slides. The task of the participant was to call out whether they thought the slide was more blue or more green in hue. While all of the slides were technically more blue than green, the hue did vary so that the decision was not immediately obvious. There were four genuine participants (the majority) and two confederates (the minority). Moscovici found that the majority group of genuine participants did indeed change their responses in line with the minority 8 per cent of the time—but only when the minority was consistent in its dissent.

Minority influence can be explained by a combination of processes that we've seen already in this book. First, the majority will implicitly know that the minority will be facing normative and informational influence pressures here, and yet they are still going against the majority—risking exclusion, ridicule, and dismissing the informational advantages of going along with the majority. What will the majority do here, when they see a consistent minority constantly banging on about their divergent point of view? Well, this is a prime example of where people engage in an attributional process (as discussed in Chapter 2). Where minorities show dissent the majority will engage in an attributional process to try to work out why the minority is behaving in the way that it is. Given that the minority is ignoring the *situational* influence (the majority), this suggests a dispositional attribution.

Of course, that dispositional attribution could be that the minority are simply 'quirky' or 'mad'. This is likely if the minority is inconsistent in its view; or when there is just one dissenter. However, when the minority, albeit small, is united, and consistent, this can lead to a dispositional attribution of *confidence*. It promotes the notion that, just maybe, the minority has some insider knowledge, or valuable insights, that put it in a privileged position relative to the majority. In short, if you want to change people's minds, then be coherent as a group, united, and consistent.

While majorities, as we have seen, typically change public but not private attitudes through normative influence, minorities stimulate greater elaboration (i.e. systematic or central route processing, as outlined by the ELM). This leads to greater scrutiny of the issue at hand. This is why encouraging dissent, 'speaking out', and diversity, is seen as healthy for group decision-making. In fact, suppressing minorities can lead to something called 'groupthink'—which can stifle creativity and lead to serious errors in judgement. Minority dissent steers people away from heuristics, encouraging *conversion* rather than simply *compliance*.

Relatedly, studies have shown that minorities promote something called divergent thinking—a particular kind of systematic thought that enables creativity and innovative thinking. The point is that simply having minorities around is useful because it stimulates more in-depth thinking and creativity, and enables multiple viewpoints to be considered. Usually this will lead to higher-quality decisions being made. For instance, studies have found that juries required to come up with a unanimous decision (rather than just a majority decision; so they have to debate and consider alternative minority opinions within the group) took longer and examined the case evidence in more detail. Even if the decision does not change to the minority view, their presence will have meant the eventual decision was the result of a more considered and careful process.

Leadership

Perhaps the ultimate minority influence is leadership—the power of one to change the attitudes, abilities, and aspirations of a group. Early research on leadership in social psychology focused on personality factors; in other words, what individual qualities make someone a good leader. For instance, studies have found that leaders have qualities like extroversion and conscientiousness rather than neuroticism. However, as well as these more general personality traits there are also different leadership styles upon which potential leaders can vary.

Three styles of leadership have been identified: autocratic, democratic, and laissez-faire. Autocratic leaders focus on creating a structured, rule-based environment and show little interest in developing relationships with members of the group. In contrast, democratic leaders develop a communal, relational structure in which group goals and objectives are decided through discussion and negotiation. Finally, laissez-faire leaders have little directive or democratic involvement with the group, leaving them to get on with the task at hand, and only getting involved if necessary.

Research has found that followers generally prefer the democratic style over the other two, because it fosters a co-operative, productive culture in which group member contributions are valued and developed. In contrast, autocratic leaders tend to foster a more aggressive, negative environment and productivity is only high when the leader is present to enforce the rules. Laissez-faire leaders are also unpopular because, while they create a positive, relaxed atmosphere, the lack of structure and focus can have a detrimental impact on productivity. Democratic leaders seem to offer the best of both worlds—the task-focused approach of autocratic leaders combined with the socio-emotional approach of laissez-faire leaders.

While the broad benefits of these three types of leadership style appear clear, research has also found that different situations can benefit from different types of leader. When leader–member relations are positive, the task is well defined, and the authority of the leader is legitimate, then socio-emotional styles like democratic and laissez-faire seem to work well. However, when the relationship between the leader and members is poor, the task ill defined, and the authority of the leader questioned, then more task-focused approaches are required.

Leader–member exchange theory goes even further than this, and suggests that leader effectiveness depends precisely on the relationship developed between the leader and followers. Thus, high-quality relationships result in trust, liking, and respect— developing an intrinsic motivation for followers to work for the group goals espoused by the leader.

According to *social identity theory* (which I'll discuss more in Chapter 5), good relations can also encourage followers to 'depersonalize'; that is, come to see themselves less as individuals and more as group members—more readily adopting the goals of the group. Similarly, leaders who have depersonalized to the core qualities of the group are seen positively because there is a good fit between their characteristics and the social identity projected by the group.

Social facilitation

As we've seen, attitudes predict behaviour (under the right conditions), but sometimes being in a group has a direct effect on behaviour that is unmediated by attitudes. The study of group processes is an area of social psychology that intersects with the sort of social influence studies discussed in this chapter, but with a greater focus on group productivity and performance.

As discussed in Chapter 1, the phenomenon of *social facilitation* was investigated in the first ever social psychology experiment. Norman Triplett was interested in whether, in the presence of others, people perform better at whatever task they do (be this athletics, music, or work-based tasks). Triplett asked his participants (who were school children) to turn fishing reels as fast as they could. In one condition the children were asked to carry out the task individually, in the other in pairs. What he found was when the children performed in pairs they turned the fishing reels far more quickly than when they were asked to do the task alone.

Subsequent research has attempted to develop theories to explain social facilitation effects. A prominent explanation is *evaluation-apprehension*. Evaluation-apprehension is not so different from normative influence—it is anxiety at the thought of being judged by a crowd. Here, however, the focus is on performance (behaviour) rather than attitude expression. The idea is that evaluation-apprehension causes heightened physiological arousal (heart rate, adrenaline, etc.), which stimulates the body to perform simple actions more quickly (e.g. clapping loudly, riding a bicycle).

This increases people's capacity to make a dominant (well-learned) response.

In support of this theory, studies have found that when audiences are blindfolded, the facilitation effect disappears. However, the effect has even been observed in animals such as insects, and chickens lay more eggs when other chickens are around. Evaluation-apprehension cannot explain social facilitation effect in animals, who presumably aren't concerned with making a good impression! Some researchers have therefore suggested that while concern about being judged may well increase physiological arousal, some arousal occurs simply through being around others—which can account for both the human and animal observations.

Arousal explanations also explain why sometimes a social facilitation effect occurs and sometimes the opposite is observed—a *social inhibition* effect. Research has found that while the presence of others enhances the *speed* with which people perform *simple* tasks, it *inhibits* task efficiency in more complex tasks. For example, in the presence of others people clap more vigorously, but are less likely to successfully complete a maths test. Since simple tasks are easy and well learned we tend to see social facilitation on these types of behaviour rather than more complex behaviours.

Strong support for the dominant response idea comes from the observation that experts show social facilitation on *complex* tasks. For instance, pool players have been found to play pool better with an audience than without, and the same can be said for many sports (performance being optimal 'on the day'). This is because for experts even complex behaviours are well learned within their domain of expertise.

However, in humans task-difficulty is not the only thing that determines whether the presence of others increases or decreases performance. The other thing is whether people are being evaluated *individually*, or whether the unit of assessment is the *group*. This distinction lies at the core of another classic social psychological phenomenon called social loafing.

Social loafing

Social loafing is a reduction in individual performance when efforts are pooled and so cannot be individually judged (in contrast, social facilitation occurs when individual output within the group setting is being assessed). The phenomenon was demonstrated in a classic study by Bibb Latané in 1979.

In Latané's study, six participants were asked to sit in a circle. Each was blindfolded and wore earphones with shouting voices being played through them. The participants' task was to shout as loudly as possible. The experimental manipulation was that they were told that they were shouting either with just one other person or within a group (in fact, it was always just the participant shouting on their own). What Latané found was that participants shouted less loudly when they believed they were shouting within a group (versus with just one other person). This social loafing phenomenon shows how our contribution can very often, literally, be 'lost in the crowd'.

Latané proposed that social loafing is a consequence of a more general phenomenon in social psychology—diffusion of responsibility. Diffusion of responsibility describes how in a group individuals are less likely to feel personally responsible for the outcome (especially if their contribution can easily get 'lost in the crowd'). Here, it explains the group dynamics when people are not individually judged for their performance in a group. Because each individual is less personally responsible, and will not be evaluated, there is less of a compulsion to perform well (as well as less evaluation-apprehension).

Diffusion of responsibility can have some serious, even life-threatening consequences. In March 1964 Kitty Genovese was walking home through Kew Gardens in Queens, New York. She was attacked by a man with a knife, and tried to fight him off while screaming for help. No one came to help, despite thirty-eight local residents admitting they heard the screams. Kitty died after being stabbed eight times. The case of Kitty Genovese stimulated a great deal of work by social psychologists to understand when people don't intervene and help in an emergency.

Latané and John Darley carried out an experimental study to try to model the processes involved in this bystander apathy effect. Participants arrived in the laboratory either on their own, or with two other participants. After a few minutes smoke started to fill the room. The research question was how long would participants wait to raise the alarm? The findings demonstrated the huge power of people to, sometimes, inhibit action. While 75 per cent of participants raised the alarm almost immediately when alone, when two other genuine participants were in the room only 38 per cent took any action. When there was a confederate who remained seated and seemed totally unconcerned with the smoke rapidly filling the room, only 10 per cent were stimulated to action.

In a subsequent study the researchers aimed to model more closely the Kitty Genovese murder, by making the emergency about someone else. Would participants help in the presence of others? They set up a situation in which a participant would hear a fellow participant in another room having an epileptic seizure (in fact, the fellow participant was a confederate and the seizure was faked). While 85 per cent of participants raised the alarm immediately when alone, only 64 per cent did when there were two others present, and only 31 per cent when they believed four others were present. This diffusion of responsibility effect has even been found to occur when people simply imagine being in the presence of others.

So that's social influence. In the next chapter I'll go on to talk about when social influence can turn bad—how obedience can lead people to commit terrible acts of cruelty, and how social events and social pressures can lead to aggression towards, and oppression of, minority groups.

Chapter 4
Obedience, oppression, and aggression

Why do good people do bad things? Continuing on from the discussion of conformity, in this chapter I'll talk about a particularly pernicious form of social influence: obedience to authority. I'll show how social power and the situation interact to compel normal people to behave in extraordinarily bad ways. I'll then extend this discussion to look more generally at the nature of social oppression. Is there is a 'prejudiced' personality, and are some people just predisposed towards aggression and intolerance towards minorities? I'll show that while some people are more prejudiced than others, this cannot explain the widespread and pervasive nature of prejudice in modern society. Rather, there are psychological processes that provide the potential for prejudice in us all. I'll show how social psychology has helped us to understand the nature of prejudice, and has provided new ways of tackling this pervasive social problem.

Obedience

In Chapter 3 we discussed Asch's classic conformity studies. We saw that people's attitudes, at least the ones they express openly, can change in response to normative influence. In other words, people sometimes go along with a group simply to avoid being excluded or left out. However, there is another, more insidious form of social influence that has revealed the darkest side of human nature: obedience to authority. Behaving in line with explicit orders (rather than implicit norms propagated by the group) can be thought of as an extreme form of conformity.

Stanley Milgram's studies of obedience are among the most famous in social psychology. This is not just because they so dramatically revealed the great impact of social influence, but also because they raised questions about ethical procedures in psychology experiments. These questions have shaped modern-day policy on what, and what should not, be allowed to happen to participants in the course of experimentation.

In Chapter 1 I talked about how much social psychology was motivated by efforts to understand the atrocities committed during World War II. Milgram's work was motivated by the strong desire to understand (and help to prevent) these most pernicious of human behaviours. Milgram was concerned with what could have driven Nazi soldiers to commit such atrocities against the Jews during the Holocaust. In particular, given that we like to believe that humans have a highly evolved sense of right and wrong, how could guards have followed orders that would result in the suffering and death of millions? At Yale University in the 1960s, Milgram set up a series of controlled experiments of obedience to attempt to answer these questions.

Just like many of the experiments described in this this book, there was a confederate and a genuine participant. In the study, which was ostensibly about learning, the participant was required to test a fellow participant on whether they had been able to successfully learn a series of word pairs. In reality, the second participant (the 'learner') was a confederate, following a script written by Milgram.

Here's how the study went. The real participant sat in one room, the confederate in another. The participant was required to read out a series of word pairs to see if the confederate learner had correctly memorized them. Questions and answers were given through an intercom. Each time the learner got a pairing wrong, the 'teacher' (who was the genuine participant) was required to give them an electric shock. The shocks were not real, but the participants believed they were, and to reinforce the deception the confederate learner followed Milgram's script: they screamed and protested with every shock that was delivered (the participant was told that the shocks also got more intense with each incorrect answer). Added to this, the confederate learner indicated at the start of the experiment that they had a heart condition (of course, they did not—this was just to increase the apparent impact, and danger, of the increasing shocks being delivered by the participant).

For each participant tested the script was the same. After getting a few word pairs correct the learner began to get them wrong. As such, the participant was required to give the learner increasingly intense electric shocks. At the 150-volt shock level the confederate learner began to protest '"Experimenter! That's all! Get me out of here...my heart's starting to bother me now. I refuse to go on!' At 180 volts the learner shouted out that he could no longer stand the pain, and at 300 volts he slumped into silence except for screams of pain with each successive shock. From 330 volts there was simply silence.

Before the study began the expectation was that most people would, on their own, begin to feel uncomfortable issuing the electric shocks to someone who was obviously in pain. What Milgram wanted to see was what would happen if an authority figure persistently ordered a participant to continue issuing the shocks. As such, all the way though, at any protest from the participant, Milgram simply replied with phrases ordering the participant to continue shocking the learner with phrases like 'please continue' or simply reiterating 'treat non-responses as incorrect'.

Now put yourself in this situation—what would you do? Most of us would like to believe we have a good sense of right and wrong, and would stand up to such orders, regardless of who was giving then. Don't forget that as far as the participants were concerned, the learner had a heart condition—continuing to shock this poor man might well end up killing him!

Beforehand Milgram carried out a survey to get baseline beliefs about how far people would go in obeying the authority figure in this study. He asked college students, middle-class adults, and psychiatrists the question. Unsurprisingly, most respondents thought participants would refuse to continue after the first protests from the learner. Psychiatrists predicted that only 0.1 per cent of people would follow Milgram's orders completely up to the maximum shock labelled '450 volts: XXX—danger severe shock' (Figure 4).

It turned out everyone was quite wrong. While 86 per cent of participants were predicted to have refused the order by 210

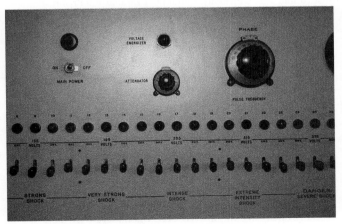

4. 'XXX—Danger severe shock!' Milgram's shock box.

volts—in fact not a single person had. 96 per cent should have refused at 315 volts (when the screaming began), but only 22.5 per cent had. 65 per cent of participants obeyed Milgram right up to the maximum 'danger severe shock' level.

Why did people obey right up to these levels? According to Bibb Latané it's all to do with social impact. According to his theory, Latané argued that social influence depends on three key factors: number, strength, and immediacy. Each of these can add power to social impact, and the analogy Latané used was of a dark room to which one gradually adds more light bulbs. So, the higher the number of light bulbs you have, the brighter the room. Regarding strength, the higher the wattage of the bulbs, the brighter the room will be. Finally, take immediacy: the closer you move a light towards a wall, the brighter will the light appear.

Social impact theory provides a framework for predicting the effects of obedience. In Milgram's study the person exerting influence was apparently a respected scientist (with a white lab coat, serious demeanour) and the study was carried out in a highly respected institution: Yale University. Remember Zimbardo's Prison Experiment from Chapter 2, where the randomly assigned participants immersed themselves in the roles of prison guard and inmates so incredibly quickly? This is similar: the perceived social role assigned to the person giving the orders afforded them a huge amount of social impact *strength*, and that meant greater social impact when it came to giving orders. Even though there was just one person giving the orders (so the social impact *number* was low), Milgram gave these orders in the same room as the participant. This meant there was high *immediacy*, further increasing the social impact. Correspondingly, subsequent studies found that obedience was dramatically reduced (to 40 per cent) when Milgram gave the orders in another room, through an intercom.

Notably, obedience was also reduced when there were pairs of learners; that is, the participant had social support. Remember the Asch conformity study from Chapter 3? There conformity dropped when social support was evident. It's the same here: the social impact number is relative, which means social support can dramatically reduce obedience.

Infrahumanization

While social impact theory describes the conditions under which authority figures can exert social influence, it doesn't explain the psychological process involved. In other words, what goes on in people's heads that allows them to follow orders that are so fundamentally in conflict with moral and ethical codes? Research on *infrahumanization* shows how people can possibly come to justify such acts to themselves.

Emotions can be divided up in to two different types: primary and secondary emotions. Primary emotions are those that both humans and animals are perceived to share; for example, *joy, surprise, fright, sadness*. Secondary emotions are more complex and seen as unique to humans, so are used to distinguish humans from animals: for example, *admiration, hope, indignation, melancholy*. Infrahumanization describes the tendency to attribute uniquely human secondary emotions to other people or groups to a lesser extent than to oneself or one's own group. Infrahumanization therefore describes the process of dehumanizing others.

Understanding infrahumanization is important because it can be used to justify treating members of particular social groups in terrible ways. This is because if one group of people is believed to be 'less than human' then it makes it easier to argue that they should not be afforded the same rights as other people. Growing evidence demonstrates the different ways in which infrahumanization has been applied to certain ethnic minorities, and how this process can serve to justify the most heinous forms of discrimination.

In 2007 Amy Cuddy and colleagues demonstrated the importance of infrahumanization for understanding reactions to a major tragedy in the US. The authors approached participants two weeks after Hurricane Katrina which hit New Orleans in August 2005, flooding 80 per cent of the city, claiming at least 1,800 victims, and leaving around 60,000 residents homeless. White, black, and Latino Americans were presented with a fictional news story about a mother who had lost a child during the hurricane. Participants were subsequently asked what emotions they thought the mother would be feeling, and whether they intended to volunteer for the Hurricane Katrina relief efforts. Cuddy and colleagues found that white participants thought the mother experienced more secondary emotions if she was identified as white than if they were identified as black. In other words, they engaged in infrahumanization on the basis of race. Furthermore, participants who didn't infrahumanize were more likely to say they intended to volunteer in the relief effort.

Other research using brain-scanning technology has found infrahumanization is related to the activation of specific brain regions. The research found that when highly stigmatized groups (i.e. drug addicts and the homeless) were described without reference to secondary emotions there was an absence of activity in the medial prefrontal cortex (mPFC)—an area associated with advanced social cognition. In fact, the mPFC was activated for a whole range of social groups *except* stigmatized minorities. In contrast, these minorities activated the insula and amygdala, which are regions that typically 'light up' when someone feels disgust. This provides a biological mechanism that explains how infrahumanization works, and how people can come to justify prejudice and intolerance towards minority groups. Infrahumanization actually leads to lower activation of brain regions normally associated with identifying and interacting with other people, and distinguishing them from non-animate objects.

Social Psychology

The authoritarian personality

Milgram's work suggested that good people can be compelled to do bad things due to social influence exerted by a powerful other. The research on infrahumanization further helps explain how they can then justify such acts of immorality to themselves. But what about the person giving the orders? Can we attribute prejudice and intolerance to just a small minority of the population who hold extreme views and ideologies and are, in turn, adept at influencing others?

Early social psychological theories were designed to try to understand how terrible events like the Holocaust could have occurred. The focus of these early theories was on the type of person who might hold extreme prejudiced views, and seek power and influence over others in their expression. Probably the most famous of these personality theories was Adorno's concept of *the authoritarian personality*.

Adorno's work was motivated by the desire to understand (and help to prevent) the atrocities of World War II. While they shared a goal, Adorno's approach was different from Milgram's. Milgram believed people obeyed immoral orders as a result of a particular constellation of factors in the context (e.g. a cultural norm where hierarchy is respected unquestioningly). In contrast, Adorno believed that such hatred could only have resided within a tiny minority, and that these 'authoritarians' were the way they were because of how they had been brought up. Like several other theories described in this book (e.g. cognitive dissonance in Chapter 3), there was a strong Freudian influence here.

According to the theory, children exposed to overly strict parenting methods come to develop a repressed hatred for authority. In line with Freudian principles of repression, because this hatred cannot be directed towards the parents (for fear of punishment), it is redirected towards weaker targets. This repressed hatred continues in to later life and is manifest in prejudice towards minority groups such as immigrants. This is because such groups are weaker social targets upon whom it is easier to release the frustration and hatred built up towards (parental) authority figures. Along with this, because the individual has learned to hide their true feelings, they end up displaying an overly deferential attitude to authority, rules, and hierarchies.

While intellectually brilliant, empirical evidence ultimately didn't support Adorno's theory. In particular, it could not account for situational, cultural, or historical variations in prejudice. For instance, some research found that while 60 per cent of Virginia miners followed racial segregation above ground, they were socially integrated below ground. In other words, the white and black co-workers would get on and show incredible camaraderie while in the mine, but as soon as they were out in wider society—where racial prejudice was rife—they would practically ignore one another. If there was such a thing as a prejudiced personality, this implies an invariant approach to thinking about groups and minorities, but here was clear moderation of behaviour due to the situation. Other research from this time found that southern US states with larger black population ratios had *stronger* anti-black attitudes but similar authoritarianism scores to states with smaller black population ratios. This variation in the culture of prejudice across states implies that a simple personality inventory is insufficient to capture the true nature of prejudice. Finally, personality theories cannot explain the nation-wide escalation of prejudice observed throughout history, such as the rapid the rise of anti-Semitism in 1930s Germany.

Although individual differences cannot explain prejudice on a societal level, clearly some people are more prejudiced than others and the theory has been valuable for developing personality theories in the social and political sciences. A contemporary example is *social dominance orientation*, a personality theory proposed by Jim Sidanius. This theory puts forward the idea that our societies are defined in part by implicit ideologies that either promote or attenuate status hierarchies, and that people can vary in the extent to which they either accept or reject these ideas.

According to Sidanius and colleagues, people who are high in social dominance orientation strongly favour social hierarchies, and will behave in ways designed to preserve and maintain the hierarchical system. Social dominance orientation has, for example, been found to predict sexism, nationalism, and ethnic prejudice against a range of different minority groups and among samples from a range of countries including the US, Canada, Mexico, Israel, Taiwan, China, and New Zealand. There is also evidence that people high in social dominance orientation support suspension of civil liberties, and are opposed to immigration and gay rights. These effects remain even after controlling for a wide range of other individual difference factors including self-esteem, need for structure, neuroticism, psychoticism, traditionalism, and several demographic factors.

While undoubtedly some people have prejudiced personalities, ultimately the concept is limited in explaining the prevalence of prejudice in modern society. This is because personality theories cannot account for the impact of context on prejudice, nor the rapid, culture-wide shifts seen historically and over time. There is, however, research that identifies more general mechanisms of the social mind that promote intolerance, prejudice, and infrahumanization. Instead of focusing on personality factors that might predict prejudice, these models identify social and cultural conditions which can trigger aggressive attitudes and behaviour.

Catharsis

According to cathartic models, everyone has the capacity to commit aggressive acts. Frustration builds and builds until it needs an outlet. When the pressure is too much, aggression is the release of this frustration. Like the authoritarian personality, Freudian psychoanalytic principles lie at the core of this idea. The best-known cathartic approach is the *frustration-aggression hypothesis* (FAH). The idea is that frustration is taken out on minority targets, who are seen as scapegoats, because they provide an easy vent for frustration.

Archival evidence for the FAH comes from a study by Hovland and Sears. They found that lynching of African Americans in the late 1800s increased when the price of cotton decreased. Low cotton prices indicated economic depression, which according to the FAH led to frustration, which in turn led to aggression. This relationship can also be observed today in the apparent link between economic hardship and calls for a tightening of immigration policy, and where social and economic deprivation have been linked to a range of conflicts around the world (such as the 1999–2001 war in the former Yugoslavia).

Although frustration can be the cause of aggression and oppression, other social psychological theories highlight alternative processes. For instance, in his *excitation-transfer model* Berkowitz suggested a cognitive priming process (see Chapter 2). So, you may be frustrated and angry from an argument you had at work, and then arrive home to snap at your partner when he or she asks how your day has been. This could be explained by displaced frustration, but it could equally be that the anger you felt at work 'primed' a more general angry state that then framed your interaction with your partner. In the same way, excitation-transfer could explain why anti-immigration sentiment increases during economic hardship, providing an alternative to the Freudian cathartic explanation.

Illusory correlation

The excitation-transfer model draws on cognitive theories rather than psychoanalytic theory. This cognitive approach also offers a further explanation for intolerance and oppression. Specifically, minority groups can be scapegoated because of the tendency of the social mind to take cognitive shortcuts. *Illusory correlation* is the belief that two variables are associated with one another when in fact there is little or no actual association. It is another manifestation of the social mind attempting to build a predictive mental model of how the world works.

In their classic experiment Hamilton and Gifford asked participants to read information about people from two fictitious groups, Group A and Group B. Group A represented the majority and Group B represented the minority. A key assumption was that people would be exposed to twice as many 'behavioural data points' for majorities than minorities, so to model this twice as many behaviours were provided to describe Group A than Group B. Importantly, while the minority Group B had half as many behaviours as the majority Group A, there were also half as many negative behaviours as positive behaviours for each group. This meant twice as much of the information *about both groups* involved positive behaviours versus negative behaviours. In other words there was no *actual* correlation between group identity and the proportion of positive versus negative information.

What Hamilton and Gifford found was that after exposure to this information, and when asked to subsequently recall the behaviours presented for both groups, participants recalled a disproportionately high number of negative behaviours for Group B than Group A. In other words, participants perceived an 'illusory' correlation between the minority group and negative behaviours.

This illusory correlation can be explained by a specific cognitive shortcut called the representativeness heuristic. Using the basic belief that things that co-occur are linked (i.e. predict each other), people make the assumption that minority groups will possess more negative behaviours. Minority groups are small; negative behaviours infrequent; therefore minority groups must also be negative.

These illusory correlations are readily apparent in the media, for instance between Muslims and terrorism, or between black people and gun crime in the US. However, illusory correlation cannot account for how negative stereotypes develop when there is *no majority* (e.g. gender stereotyping). This is where learning theories come in.

Associative learning

We saw in Chapter 3 how people can readily learn to associate positive and negative feelings towards national groups. The same process can also explain the intergenerational transmission of stereotypes, through hearing minorities discussed in negative terms in childhood. If one constantly hears, from parents, friends, or on TV, negative traits and expectations being paired with particular category labels (be that male, female, black, Muslim, Polish, or even generic words like 'immigrant' or 'asylum seeker') then this can lead associations to be formed. It is really just the same as how this highly adaptive mechanism helps us learn any other association (e.g. the patterns of movement needed to ride a bicycle). This is a case of overapplication of an adaptive mechanism that contributes to a problematic social issue.

If these learning principles apply, people should be found to automatically think of more positive associations with names of people from their own group, and more negative associations with names of people from minority or stigmatized groups. One of the most frequently used measures of associative attitudes is the *implicit association test* (IAT). This is a task that identifies the speed with which participants can categorize positive or negative words alongside own-group or other-group names or faces. It typically reveals an own-group favouring bias. Specifically, people find it easier to associate their own group (compared to other groups) with positive words, and other groups (compared to the one's own group) with negative words.

The IAT has identified own-group favouring bias on the basis of gender, race, and religion, and IAT scores have been found to predict racial discrimination in terms of slurs, physical harm, and recommended budget cuts to Jewish, Asian, and black student organizations. Studies even have shown this effect in the most basic forms of human language. Generic designators referring to one's own group (e.g. 'we', 'us', 'our') facilitate subsequent response times to positive words compared to words like 'they', 'them', or 'their'.

System justification theory

As well as influencing attitudes towards minority groups, the social mind's drive to create a predictive model of how the world works can serve to maintain minority group discrimination once it is established. According to John Jost's *system justification theory* the social mind's tendency to seek order and stability is manifest in a strong psychological motive to defend and justify the status quo, and this tendency compels people to support ideologies like social dominance orientation. In particular, groups high up in a society's status hierarchy will be compelled to maintain and justify the status quo, and this is manifest through disinclinations to change existing political systems, or the use of 'complementary stereotypes' (e.g. justifying gender inequality by elevating women as homemakers above women as business leaders).

An interesting implication of the theory is that sometimes even disadvantaged groups will be motivated to maintain the status quo—preferring to maintain their own disadvantaged but stable position in a status hierarchy, rather than initiate social change that will introduce uncertainty into the system. The theory helps explain why social change is sometimes slow to take effect, or why collective action is difficult to establish in response to inequality and injustice.

There is growing evidence for system justification theory. For instance, studies have shown that people tend to perceive the status quo as preferable in terms of current political power, public funding priorities, and gender inequality. When system justification motives are in operation there tends to be a greater perception that ethnic groups differ from one another, heightened minority scapegoating, support for greater restriction of civil liberties (ID cards, incarceration without trial), and greater endorsement of a strong immigration policy and anti-terror laws.

Terror management theory

Another drive that can compel people to support oppression and inequality is outlined by *terror management theory* (TMT). The idea is that humans, like all animals, have a strong survival instinct. Unlike other animals, however, we also possess the intellectual capacity to realize that one day we will die—a fact that can paralyse us with fear at the prospect of our own mortality. Think of it like a huge threat to the social mind's desire to find meaning and structure to the world. According to TMT the recognition that some day we will die, cease to exist, and return to nothing, creates an existential terror that threatens to undermine our sense of meaningful existence.

TMT argues that adopting a cultural ideology (i.e. a set of values, for example religious beliefs and social norms) provides a sense of structure and meaning to our social universe and enables us to maintain the belief that our lives are meaningful and significant. Being part of a culture with beliefs, values, and laws effectively buffers us from this mortality terror, giving us an ability to 'live on' after our own death (through the perceived continuity of that way of life). While system justification theory can be seen as the manifestation of the social mind's desire for stability and structure in the here and now, TMT can be seen as the manifestation of this drive over time, stretching out even after our own death.

So cultural worldviews are important because they allow us to transcend death, either literally, through a belief in an afterlife, or symbolically, through lasting cultural achievements. If belief in our cultural continuity provides protection against existential terror, then reminding someone of their mortality should increase their need to endorse and support that worldview, and therefore stimulate efforts to protect it from violation. This can lead to support for extreme aggression against other groups and cultures in an effort to protect one's own cultural worldview. TMT therefore has clear relevance for understanding why people sometimes engage in extreme actions to protect their worldview (for instance, acts of terrorism).

Terrorism

Societies struggling with oppression, inequality, and relative deprivation can often fall prey to terrorism. Social psychology can provide some insights into how individuals can be led through the stages that gradually and eventually lead them to commit atrocious acts of violence. Moghaddam proposed the 'stairway to terrorism', a metaphor that outlines five 'floors' that an individual gradually moves through when they are radicalized.

The ground floor is the perception of relative deprivation, inequality, poverty, and injustice propagated by privileged sections of society. These conditions lay the groundwork for progressing to the first floor, which is when an individual attempts to use legitimate channels to effect social change (i.e. protest, appealing to governments). If the individual becomes frustrated with attempts to change the status quo this will, through catharsis, lead to a displacement of aggression where others are blamed as the source of this frustration. This is the second level. On the third floor the individual gets recruited to a terrorist organization, adopts an alternative moral code, and comes to see mainstream society as immoral. On the fourth floor the individual is encouraged to engage in infrahumanization,

5. The radicalization process can ultimately lead to an act of terrorism.

coming to see all members of the mainstream society as less than human. This enables them to move to the fifth stage, where because civilian targets are perceived as non-human, moral and ethical rules are suspended and a terrorist act is carried out (Figure 5).

This stairway metaphor suggests that the root cause of terrorist acts is social inequality, deprivation, and the psychological processes that are then engaged by the social mind to deal with the social, cognitive, and existential dissonance this causes. The frustration with the lack of ability to change the system leads ultimately to the terrorist act, but in this the cycle is self-perpetuating. Terrorist acts are precisely the sort of system threat that lead people to bolster their support for the status quo. This is because by definition they suggest the cultural, social, and political system in which the individual resides (and by extension the mind's social universe) is unstable, unsecure, and unpredictable. In this way terrorist acts threaten the social mind's need to establish predictability and stability, which in turn makes the status quo even more difficult to change, which in turn sets new individuals on the road to radicalization.

How then to break this cycle? Social psychologists have argued that to address the issues and problems described in this chapter ultimately we require an analysis that takes in to account the *relationship* between different groups in society. In Chapter 5, we explore these theories of intergroup relations. These theories encompass the perceived relationships between the individual, their own group, and other groups, and in so doing provide a range of psychological approaches for preventing prejudice, and for promoting more positive intergroup relations.

Chapter 5
Intergroup relations

The social psychology we've studied so far has helped us understand why we have a world in which prejudice, stereotyping, and social exclusion remain pervasive problems. Cognitive biases like heuristics lead to illusory correlation, so that minority groups (like Muslims or immigrants) are seemingly linked with occurrences of bad things like terrorism and economic recession. We've seen how frustration can turn to aggression that needs to be released, and how minority groups are the 'easy option' for this cathartic process. We've also seen how a few people have prejudiced personalities, and how through social influence processes they can compel others to conform to their worldview, or if they are in leadership positions, even compel others to obey orders that are immoral and wrong.

All of these psychological processes can give rise to inequality, intolerance, and exclusion; however, they tell only half the story. To fully understand the dynamics of social conflict, we need to consider not just the individual's perception of other groups, but their perception of their own group *in relation to* other groups. In other words, we need to adopt what's called an intergroup perspective. Recognizing that individuals self-categorize as members of a particular group, and adopt an 'intergroup mindset' (that is, thinking in terms of intergroup competition rather than taking a personal perspective) has profound implications for our understanding of intergroup relations. These implications were first identified by Musaf Sherif in a programme of pivotal studies in social psychology.

The summer camp studies

As well as providing seminal work on social influence (see Chapter 3), Sherif also provided some classic studies that set the scene for the next sixty years of research on intergroup conflict. Rather than looking at *intra*group processes, which is what much of the work on social influence is all about, this time Sherif turned his attention to *inter*group processes. Intergroup processes focus on how comparisons between one's own group and other groups affect attitudes and behaviour, particularly with respect to prejudice, intolerance, and conflict.

Sherif proposed that animosity between groups has at its core a 'realistic' conflict of interest. In other words, he believed that conflict was rather rational, the result of being a naïve scientist. According to his *realistic group conflict theory*, prejudice and hostility has at its root competition for scarce resources: the scarcer the resource, the greater the animosity and conflict.

On the face of it this seems to make sense. Conflicts of interest between groups abound (e.g. former Yugoslavia, Northern Ireland, the Middle East), and in all these cases the conflict revolves around (at least in part) competition over land, or resources like oil. It can also explain anti-immigration sentiment, and how this appears to increase during times of economic recession (i.e. lack of jobs can be indicative of a scarcity of resource).

To test this theory Sherif devised a series of quasi-experimental longitudinal studies, carried out at the Robbers Cave State Park in Oklahoma in the 1950s. Sherif was capitalizing on a North American tradition where groups of eleven- to twelve-year-olds (in this case all boys) head off for a few weeks each summer to camps to engage in a range of activities like canoeing, climbing, and other competitive sports. Sherif realized that this long-standing American tradition could provide an ideal setting in which to observe intergroup behaviour from inception to dissolution. In so doing he could avoid a range of confounding influences associated with studying established social groups, such as political, economic, and historic factors, all of which can obscure the psychological process at work. It was the perfect 'Petri dish' in which to test how competition influences intergroup conflict.

The study involved three stages. In Stage 1 the boys had just arrived at the camp and knew nothing of each other. The first thing that happened was that they were placed, on a purely random basis, into two groups for the remainder of the two weeks at the camp (such camps are based on team competition and this division into arbitrary groups suited the interests of the researchers perfectly). On doing this, Sherif immediately observed spontaneous suggestions for competition between the two groups, spontaneous social comparisons and the development of group icons. That is to say, as soon as the group of boys was split in two, and allocated different group labels, they began to suggest that the two groups compete against each other. They began to throw verbal taunts at each other (along the lines of, 'Your group sucks!'). One group called themselves the 'Rattlers' and the other the 'Eagles' (Figure 6). Interestingly, within a short time the boys in the respective groups had made some icons to represent the animal name of their group, and put them above their (separate) dormitory huts. This was a first indication of the development of a 'social' identity.

Having observed this immediate impact of group division, at Stage 2 Sherif introduced what he believed might be a key factor in the emergence of intergroup conflict. Again, he took advantage of a typical element of the summer camp experience: competitive games between the groups. The resources in

6. Group formation led to spontaneous suggestions of competition in Sherif's summer camp study.

question were prized rewards such as medals and penknives. These games, including baseball and tug-of-war, led to a dramatic rise in tension between the groups, culminating in one group even physically attacking the other's icon. One night one group even burned the other's flag and ransacked their cabin! It seemed that the intergroup context had come to dominate the behaviour of the boys, so much so that interpersonal thinking was almost entirely suppressed. By this point 93 per cent of the boys' friendships were found to lie within the boundaries of their group.

At Stage 3 Sherif was interested in seeing whether introducing cooperative goals could reduce conflict. The researchers arranged for the boys' bus to break down on their way back from the morning's activity. They arranged it so that only if the two groups worked together would they be able to push start the bus (and get back in time for lunch). Cooperation between the groups did indeed lead to a reduction in observed conflict between the groups.

Sheriff's summer camp studies were hugely influential. They were the first time that anyone had attempted to systematically examine the behavioural consequences of group competition. Importantly, the research showed that personality differences are not necessary for intergroup conflict whereas *competition* can be a sufficient condition. This work moved research on from an individual focus or interpersonal framework to an *intergroup* perspective.

So does this mean all conflict can be traced back to competition for resources? In Sheriff's studies, spontaneous derogation of the other group occurred at Stage 1, but all that had happened was that the boys had been divided into two groups. This suggests that categorization alone—simply becoming aware of group differences—might be enough to incite intergroup conflict. Some years later the idea that merely being categorized could lead to conflict was addressed experimentally in what would become one of the most influential experiments ever carried out in social psychology.

The minimal group paradigm

In Bristol, England, in the 1970s Henri Tajfel was a social psychologist interested in understanding the origins of conflict. As a prisoner of war during World War II, Tajfel witnessed first hand the potential of social categories to provide the basis for terrible atrocities. His drive to understand how simple social labels could underlie such atrocities led him to develop what has become one of the most important and influential studies of social categorization in the field of social psychology.

Tajfel developed an experimental technique he called the *minimal group paradigm* (MGP). The MGP creates an ad hoc (or 'minimal') basis for categorization and includes measures of discrimination between, and evaluation of, the groups involved. In Tajfel's original experiment the participants, who were schoolchildren, were allocated to two groups on an arbitrary basis (rather like they were in Sherif's summer camp studies). Participants were shown a number of slides of paintings by Paul Klee or Wassily Kandinsky—two abstract painters. They were then asked to record how much they liked each of the paintings. On the basis of these preferences participants were ostensibly allocated to one of two minimal groups—the 'Klee' group or the 'Kandinsky' group. This feedback was, however, contrived by the experimenter, and allocation to groups was in fact completely random.

In the next phase of the experiment participants used allocation matrices to assign points to their own group (the 'ingroup') and the other group ('outgroup') members. Participants were free to use any criteria they wished in their allocations. The points were allocated via a series of decision matrices on which participants indicated with a cross through one column how much the ingroup and how much the outgroup member should receive.

There are two other key criteria that are critical for interpreting behaviour in the MGP. First, the personal identities of people in the groups were unknown—identification was by individual code number and group membership alone. All that distinguished one person from another on the decision matrices was a random code number (e.g. person number: '419') and their group membership (e.g. 'Klee' or 'Kandinsky'). This meant that the only possible basis for making any differential allocation was group membership, as personal histories, attitudes, or impressions were simply not available.

Second, participants could not allocate points to themselves. This meant that participants would not gain personally from point allocations, so there was no competition for resource, so no link between ingroup allocations and self gain. In other words, any differential allocation observed would indicate that something other than Sherif's 'rational' economic explanation was going on.

What Tajfel and colleagues observed was a persistent tendency for participants to allocate more points to people in their own group compared to people in the other group. Mere categorization was therefore sufficient to elicit intergroup bias. Take a moment to consider what this means. Tajfel found here a tendency to favour one's own group over another even when the group identities were meaningless. There was no past interaction, no history of conflict, and not a single bit of self-interest.

The unique characteristic of this MGP was that the groups really did represent the most basic form of social categorization. Unlike real social groups defined by nationality, religion, or age, there was no economic imbalance, political motivation, or past interaction associated with these groups. This finding suggested that if you strip away all the economic, political, and historical factors that appear to aggravate intergroup conflict, at its foundation lies a psychological core—a persistent tendency to favour 'us' over 'them'.

While groundbreaking, Tajfel's original study was not quite completely minimal. Critics argued that it was not mere categorization that was the only thing left to explain bias, but the inference of belief similarity. In other words, participants could have inferred that people who were in the same group as them also liked the same abstract paintings and that this could generalize to other personality traits. In short, they may have inferred that the people who shared their preference for abstract paintings might be similar to them in other ways, and therefore be someone they would like.

To address this Billig and Tajfel carried out an 'ultra-minimal' group study. This time they compared the original MGP categorization on the basis of 'liking of paintings' to categorization on the basis of a simple coin toss. If the mere categorization effect really exists, then there should still be bias even in the coin toss condition. This is precisely what happened. Belief similarity did increase bias, suggesting that, like competition, it is an exacerbating factor. However, bias was still present in the coin toss condition, supporting the assertion that mere categorization lies at the core of intergroup bias.

The mere categorization effect

The *mere categorization effect* has been replicated many times using many different ways to categorize people and many different measures of evaluation. The finding is important because it suggests that there is a psychological core to prejudice, beyond the economic, political, or historical. If, however, there is a psychological process underlying the use of social categorization as a basis for prejudice and intolerance, what could it be?

A clue was provided from Tajfel's original MGP studies. One interesting aspect to these studies was that participants were given different versions of the 'matrices' used to award points in the study. These matrices were made up of a series of columns which allowed participants to give different amounts to the ingroup and the outgroup member. Importantly, participants had to choose just one box, which meant the number of points they gave to the ingroup and the outgroup were not independent; the relative amounts were fixed depending upon which box was chosen. Tajfel did this because it allowed him to explore not simply the overall number of points awarded to the ingroup and outgroup, but to test which of a range of allocation *strategies* participants used.

To illustrate, lets say box 1 contained 25 points for the ingroup member and 21 points for the outgroup member. Furthermore, lets say box 2 contained 7 points for the ingroup member and 1 point for the outgroup member. If the participant chose box 1 (25/21) over box 2 (7/1) this would demonstrate a maximal ingroup profit strategy. This is because the participant is choosing the box that awarded the most points to the ingroup.

That's straightforward, but participants could have chosen box 2 (7/1). Choosing box 2 would indicate that participants were not concerned with maximizing profit, but rather maximizing the *difference* in points allocated to the ingroup and the outgroup. This is because although box 1 would give the ingroup 25 points, it would also give the outgroup 21 points, leaving the ingroup with only 4 points more than the outgroup. In contrast, a choice of box 2 sacrifices maximal profit for the ingroup (i.e. box 1 would have provided 25 points for the ingroup, but box 2 only provides 7). However, crucially, choosing box 2 creates a larger *difference* between the ingroup and outgroup (7 minus 1 = 6 points).

Sure enough, Tajfel found a pervasive tendency for participants to choose box 2 over box 1, indicating a maximal differentiation strategy. In other words, for people in Tajfel's study it was more important to have more points *than the outgroup* than to simply have more points. This is one of the findings that revealed the true power of social context in framing people's behaviour. We don't just want resource, we want to be different from others, even if that means sacrificing overall gains.

Maximal differentiation can be explained by the *category differentiation model*. According to this model, we tend to think of all people who are in the same category as being *similar* to one another. Correspondingly we also have an automatic tendency to think of all people who are in different categories as being *different* from one another. This has the advantage of simplifying things so that information about people in the immediate context can be more efficiently processed, enabling judgements to be made more easily and with less effort. This implicit motivation can explain the mere categorization effect. Specifically, people have a desire to create simple and distinct representations of their social environment. However, in the MGP the groups are so similar to one another that the only way they can do this is by allocating more points to one group compared to another group. By doing so, they are able to accentuate the differences

Social Psychology

between people in the two categories, creating a clear two-category system.

Category differentiation can be seen as the social mind once again attempting to impose order, structure, and meaning on its social environment. This is precisely the point of category differentiation in the MGP: it enables participants to deal with the uncertain situation. Participants sacrifice self-gain just to make their group seem more different from an opposing group. In so doing they satisfy the motivation to make the world as simple and easy to predict as possible.

Category differentiation clarifies and defines social situations, providing a means for predicting how outgroupers will behave, and providing a set of prescriptive ingroup norms to guide perceivers. As such, group members will be motivated to maintain the certainty and clarity that category differentiation provides (or to reduce uncertainty when it is threatened). Consistent with this idea, many studies have shown that threat to category 'systems' leads to negative and sometimes aggressive reactions (see the discussion of system justification theory in Chapter 4). For instance, in some of my own studies I've compared responses of participants who were asked to simply evaluate the British and the French with an experimental group who were asked to read a paragraph advocating the dissolution of member states into a 'United States of Europe'. These studies found that in the latter condition bias was highest, particularly for participants for whom being British was an important part of their identity.

While the category differentiation mechanism accounts for people wanting their groups to be distinctive and differentiated, there is one tendency observed in the MGP that it finds hard to explain. If all that matters to groups is distinctiveness, why not achieve this by giving the *other* group more points? In the MGP differentiation was found to be ingroup-favouring (i.e. choosing boxes that award 7 to the ingroup and 1 to the outgroup, rather than 1 to the ingroup and 7 to the outgroup). The category differentiation model cannot explain this tendency to differentiate in favour of one's own group.

To account for this finding Tajfel and John Turner proposed *social identity theory*. This theory proposes that as well as the general desire to achieve clarity, structure, and predictability through category differentiation, we also use groups to boost our self-esteem. Think about sources of pride: your school's or university's achievements, the status of the company you work for, or how good you feel when the football team you support wins a game. We don't only feel good about our individual successes, but vicariously enjoy the success of the groups to which we belong.

Robert Cialdini called this 'basking in reflected glory'. He coined the term after observing the different types of behaviour that football team supporters exhibited after a win versus after a loss. Compared to losing a match, following a win football supporters were more likely to wear the scarves, hats, and other regalia associated with their team—and to do so for much longer. Cialdini also observed a heightened frequency of winning supporters using collective pronouns ('We won! They lost!') instead of person pronouns like 'I' or 'me'.

All this demonstrates basking in reflected glory—purposefully self-categorizing as an ingroup member to garnish the positive feelings that surround one's group. In fact, people expect their groups to furnish them with positive self-esteem from the get go. Think back to the group categorization phase in Sherif's summer camp studies, how group icons were created as soon as the groups were allocated. The desire to create positive feeling even makes people actively try to boost the positivity of their group, relative to other groups; and this is precisely what happens in the MGP. As such, while category differentiation forms the basis for discrimination, it is the desire to acquire a positive social identity that provides the motivation to favour one's own group over the other.

Reducing prejudice

Recall Stage 3 of Sherif's summer camp studies, discussed earlier in this chapter. Sherif found that cooperation reduced bias between the two groups of boys. It turns out that this demonstration signified one of the most powerful methods for promoting tolerance to be subsequently developed by social psychologists. The common ingroup identity model argues that cooperation between groups leads to 'recategorization'—a cognitive process whereby people move from representing the context as involving two distinct groups ('us' versus 'them') to being represented as a single, inclusive 'common ingroup'.

The argument is that if categorization is so pervasive as a means of organizing our social universe, then there is little point in trying to stop people doing it (in fact there are studies that show when you try to get people to suppress their stereotypes, they simply 'rebound' again later on). After all, as we've seen they are an extremely efficient and easy way of predicting how people will behave. However, just because we can't stop people using categorization this doesn't mean we can't redirect the way in which they use it. The argument is that cooperation works because it gets people to change the focus of their tendency to categorize. So, rather than focusing on 'us' versus 'them', it gets people to categorize at a more inclusive level: 'we'.

There is a great deal of evidence for the notion that cooperative interaction (the establishment of common goals) can increase people's tendency to abandon categorization at the 'us' versus 'them' level and instead adopt a common ingroup identity. In one published variant of Tajfel's MGP participants either sat round tables in a segregated pattern (AAABBB) or an integrated pattern (ABABAB). They were given distinct group names, or provided with a common name for all participants, or they were given individual 'nicknames'. In their two groups, single combined group, or as individuals, they then had to carry out a problem-solving exercise that required either a segregated group decision, or an aggregated group decision, or decisions per individual.

What the researchers found was that, compared to the two-groups condition, intergroup bias was reduced in both the aggregated group condition and the individuals group condition. Interestingly however, bias was reduced in the aggregated group condition in a different way to the individuals condition. In the aggregate group condition bias was reduced by an *increase* in the attractiveness of former outgroup members. In contrast, in the individuals condition bias reduced by a *decrease* in the attractiveness of former ingroup members. This is because recategorization works by bringing the former outgroup member into a more inclusive common ingroup. In contrast, *individuation* works by encouraging people to abandon categorization as a way of structuring the context at hand (so ingroup members no longer seem more similar and so more attractive).

Further studies have replicated the positive and unique effects of forming a common ingroup identity, and shown that it is not only cooperation that makes it happen. Studies have shown that getting people to wear the same-coloured lab coats, use the same-coloured pens, or even simply coming up with things in common, can lead to the formation of a common ingroup identity (and reduce intergroup bias). The findings also resonate with and explain practical approaches to reducing bias. Field experiments have shown that when classroom tasks are designed to promote cooperative interdependence instead of reinforcing divides (e.g. in terms of race or gender), this leads to greater tolerance and less bias. This is because such tasks reduce the salience of existing group differences, and in so doing increase the salience of a common ingroup identity.

The contact hypothesis

The idea that getting groups to work together can counteract the social mind's tendency to categorize and differentiate, and so establish more positive intergroup relations, was the focus of a seminal idea from Gordon Allport that he named *the contact hypothesis*. Allport's idea was that contact would only decrease conflict under certain conditions (e.g. when contact takes the form of a cooperative interaction). A great deal of research on those conditions has produced a roadmap for how successful strategies to promote positive intergroup relations could work. There are four key criteria.

First, social norms favouring equality must be in place. In other words, there must be social and institutional support for the aim of reducing prejudice and promoting an integrated, cohesive society. As such, the social conditions (government policy, schools, laws) should all promote integration. There are good psychological reasons why this condition is so important—because it taps into one of the most basic mechanisms in the social mind's drive towards stability and structure.

Remember cognitive dissonance theory from Chapter 3? When attitudes are not in line with behaviour this causes an unpleasant internal state, and people are motivated to avoid this dissonance. They are therefore compelled to change their attitudes to be in line with their behaviour. It follows that social policy and law-making that prevents discrimination should eventually lead to attitude change.

Take wearing seat belts in the back seats of cars. When the UK law was introduced in 1991 many people thought it was an example of the 'nanny state' encroaching in to people's personal lives. However, these days few people would disagree with the need to wear seatbelts. This is a good example of how attitudes change over time in response to new laws. The same process may well occur with regard to racial abuse and discrimination laws: eventually they may gain widespread support through a process of cognitive dissonance reduction. In practical terms, to meet this institutional support condition, workshops designed to promote more positive intergroup relations could be introduced and managed by a figure of local authority (e.g. a teacher in a classroom-based activity).

The second condition required for successful contact is *acquaintance potential*. Research has found that contact must be of sufficient frequency, duration, and intimacy to allow for the development of meaningful intergroup relations. This could be practically achieved by ensuring that groups are required to work together in cross-categorized ways (e.g. a 'jigsaw classroom'). This would ensure that category boundaries don't come to define friendships (as they did in Sherif's summer camp studies).

Third, contact must occur under conditions of equal social status. If minority groups have contact with majority group members as subordinates then this may well perpetuate negative feeling of inferiority. Each group member should therefore have an equal share of responsibility. This would ensure there is no diffusion of responsibility (or 'social loafing', see Chapter 3).

Finally, contact must be in the form of cooperative interaction. As we saw with Sherif's summer camp studies it was cooperation that was necessary for reductions in conflict to be observed. Cooperation is even more effective when it is characterized by mutual interdependence, with the team product gaining a team reward. Ensuring the outcome is of mutual interest and benefit to all members maximizes the potential for participants from both groups to form a common ingroup identity.

A contact caveat

Contact is one of the most extensively researched ideas in psychology. There have now been over 500 studies revealing a robust, highly significant, and positive relationship between contact and tolerance. However, there is a caveat to its effectiveness. Yes it works, under the right conditions, and once you get groups together; but what about when there is no *opportunity* for contact? For instance, in the US white people typically live in neighbourhoods that are made up of a small percentage of black residents. In Northern Ireland very few children attend mixed Catholic–Protestant schools. Then there is the Green Line in Cyprus and the West Bank barrier in Israel. It seems that in many of the places where contact is needed the most there is the least opportunity for it to occur.

A solution to this problem may be found in the application of mental imagery techniques to intergroup relations. Research in all areas of psychology has found mental imagery to elicit emotions that approximate to the real experience, and imagining carrying out a behaviour employs the same neurological pathways as the behaviour itself. Mental imagery techniques are also widely used by applied psychologists in a variety of domains. For instance, there are imagery techniques designed to help athletes reach peak performance, systematic desensitization techniques used by clinical psychologists to tackle phobias, ones that help promote a healthy lifestyle through diet and exercise, and educational techniques employed to enhance academic achievement.

Research on imagined contact provides a way of initiating intergroup contact where direct face-to-face contact is difficult to achieve in practice. The idea is that mentally simulating a positive contact experience approximates the thoughts and feelings associated with contact itself, leading participants to feel more comfortable and less apprehensive about the prospect of future contact with the group, which in turn should reduce negative outgroup attitudes and expectations.

Research has supported this idea: imagined contact has been found to reduce intergroup bias and encourage intentions to engage in future contact. Notably, studies have shown it enhances the availability of positive contact scripts and schemas (see Chapter 2). This suggests that imagery techniques are useful because they tap directly into the social mind's desire to make a mental model of how the world works. Guided imagined contact can mean the model is built not on negative stereotypes and expectations, but on the prospect of positive social relations. Imagined contact is therefore a good example of how understanding the basic mechanisms of the social mind can help us develop strategies—based on theory and research—that can make the world a better place.

Pro-social behaviour

The research on imagined contact demonstrates the power of promoting positive mental scripts—tapping directly into, and capitalizing on, the social mind's desire to make mental models of social relations. This idea may hold the key to not only encouraging more positive intergroup relations, but also more pro-social and pro-community behaviour too.

In one study female participants were asked to interact with a friendly woman (a confederate) in a study on 'social interaction'. As the women left the laboratory at the end of the study they were asked if they would make a pledge to give blood. When the confederate was asked first, and signed up to give blood, 67 per cent of participants also agreed to give blood. In contrast, when the participant was asked first, only 25 per cent agreed to give blood.

This research can be seen as evidence for the social mind forming a directed, positive behavioural script. Indeed, there are more contemporary examples demonstrating the power of vicariously viewed pro-social acts on pro-social behaviour. For instance, in one study participants were asked to play a pro-social video game in which players must save small animals from falling off a cliff.

After playing the game, participants reported decreased accessibility of antisocial thoughts, and showed a reduced likelihood of rating ambiguous behaviour as aggressive. Related research has found children who played pro-social video games were more likely to help, rather than harm, another participant on a subsequent task.

In sum, research on viewing pro-social acts demonstrates support for the notion that vicarious media experiences can encourage the social mind to make more positive mental scripts. These scripts can then become cognitively available when making subsequent relevant judgements or enacting relevant future behaviours. In so doing they promote a more positive pro-social orientation for the individual in general. This and related work on applied social psychology is developing new training techniques that can be applied in government, schools, and business to help encourage a more positive, harmonious, and tolerant society.

Chapter 6
Love and other attractions

This book—and social psychology in general—is in many ways all about relationships. Throughout I've talked about our relationships with others: strangers, society, groups, and collectives. We've talked about how we explain the behaviour of others (Chapter 2), how others change our attitudes (Chapter 3), how people can be intolerant or aggressive towards others (Chapter 4), and how we can encourage more positive relationships between groups (Chapter 5). Of course, in all these cases the people we're talking about could be friends, lovers, or acquaintances, but I haven't really focused on this sort of relationship in depth. In this final chapter, I delve into this most basic, and perhaps most influential, social relationship of all—the interpersonal relationship.

Ostracism

Why are we drawn to one another? As social animals humans have evolved a biological need to form bonds with others. There is no better demonstration of this than the observation of what happens when affiliation is denied or taken away. *Ostracism* describes the social process that involves exclusion from a social group. It could be anything from being left out, teased, or bullied at school, to being shunned by work colleagues on a night out, to being 'unfriended' on Facebook.

We all know that ostracism feels bad, but what social psychology experiments have revealed is the incredibly broad extent of its impact. It's not just friends, loved ones, or colleagues who can make us feel bad when they exclude us. Research has shown that even if we don't know the person, or can't even see them, exclusion makes us feel bad.

This has been demonstrated in online discussion studies, or with specially designed computer games. In one study, Williams and Jarvis asked people to play a game called Cyberball (Figure 7). In this game, three cartoon characters on the screen throw a ball to one another (each one of the cartoon characters is apparently operated by a participant in a different room—in fact there is only one real participant and the two other cartoon characters' behaviour is programmed by computer). After a short while in which the computer controlled characters throw the ball to each other, including the real participant, something changes. The computer characters gradually reduce the number of times they pass the ball to the participant and eventually stop throwing it to them altogether. This exclusion had a huge effect on participants— they subsequently reported lowered self-esteem and a reduced sense of having a 'meaningful existence'. It is hard to believe this simple

Player 1

Player 3

Player 2

7. **Cyberball's cartoon characters.**

and banal game could have such an effect on participants. One could imagine the negative effects if one was excluded by a friend or partner, but a cartoon character apparently controlled by a stranger in another room?

It gets even weirder: even when participants were told that the cartoon characters were controlled by computer, participants felt just as bad. It seems we are simply unable to switch off the part of our brains that controls our response to being excluded. Other demonstrations go further and show that if we dislike or *despise* the person or group doing the ostracizing, we still feel bad. For instance, one study showed that even being ostracized by the Klu Klux Klan led to all the negative feelings associated with ostracism.

What could explain such universal and extreme responses to being excluded? Well, our need to affiliate is one of the most basic manifestations of the social mind, helping us to create a predictive and meaningful model of the world around us. Supporting the idea that this desire goes right back to the evolution of the human mind, ostracism has a deep visceral reaction that mirrors the experience of real pain. Recent brain imaging studies show that when people are ostracized the same part of their brain 'lights up' as if they were experiencing physical pain. In other words, the social 'pain' of being excluded leads to exactly the same physiological reaction as inflicting physical harm.

This suggests that we are actually hardwired to avoid the social pain of ostracism in the same way as we are hardwired to avoid physically damaging ourselves. This is because from an evolutionary standpoint humans are stronger and more productive when they can pool their skills in groups, tribes, colonies, and collectives. For our ancestors, the prospect of being excluded—and so having to fend and fight for themselves—may have been *the* most dangerous threat to survival there was. Think of dental pain and how it can be seen as an evolved, adaptive mechanism that makes sure we look after our teeth (once our ancestors lost their teeth, they'd starve). In the same way our bodies and mind tell us we need other people to survive, so we are adapted to feel actual pain when the threat of ostracism occurs. This helps explain why humans are such a social species, and have such a strong capacity for affiliation with others.

Affiliation

So we have an in-built desire to affiliate—but what determines *who* we affiliate with? While we are born with some affiliations (ethnicity, nationality, gender) others we choose (friends, lovers). So when we have a choice, what makes us want to affiliate with one person or another?

A key determinant is similarity. Research has shown that birds of a feather do indeed flock together, whether this is in terms of physical characteristics, interests, values, religion, personality, or background. Studies have found that when participants read a set of questionnaire responses, those that indicated attitudes that aligned with the participant's own view were liked more than those that indicated dissimilar attitudes. This can be seen as the social mind creating a stable and predictive model of their social environment. People who are similar to us are more predictable. This is because we know how we behave ourselves, so can infer that someone similar will also behave like us in particular situations. To predict the behaviour of a similar other we have the best template possible—ourselves!

The way that similarity signals predictability may be so ingrained that it's become a heuristic itself. According to the *matching hypothesis*, people believe that those similar in attractiveness will be happier together (Figure 8). Heider's *balance theory* of social relations argues that similarity is valuable because it enables a sense of social harmony to be attained. Thus, if two people like the same sort of movies, then there will be lower likelihood of

"Hey, opposites attract."

8. Do opposites attract? Studies show that similarity is actually a more powerful predictor of attraction.

arguments when deciding where to go out. From an evolutionary perspective, this also reflects a critical survival instinct. Someone who shares our attitudes are more likely to fight with us, than against us.

The process is dynamic, as we saw with the studies of cognitive dissonance in Chapter 3. So when attitudes are out of line with behaviour then this can cause an unpleasant dissonance. This dissonance can be removed by changing the attitude to be in line with the behaviour. This can also occur between people in the maintenance of relationships. If two people are having a disagreement, then often they don't just agree to disagree but one can often change their views to come in line with the other—balance and harmony is then restored.

Anxiety

Following the 9/11 terrorist attacks in New York researchers attached digital voice recorders to the clothes of participants. In the ten days following the attacks, they found that people moved from making telephone conversations to being much more likely to have face-to-face conversations. This seemed to be a coping mechanism, designed to help them deal with the stress of the attacks.

This observational study supports experimental research that has identified shared anxiety as a stimulus for affiliation. For example, in one study people were told they would be receiving painful electric shocks as part of the procedure. After being informed of this (something one would expect to be anxiety-provoking) the participants were given a choice as to whether they'd like to wait alone in a private waiting room, or in a communal waiting room with other participants. Sixty-three per cent chose to wait with other participants rather than alone, suggesting that anxiety makes us seek out social support.

This makes sense when we consider the benefits of social support that we've seen already. Recall Asch's conformity study, or Milgram's obedience study. In both cases social support was the key to participants' ability to stand up to others. Here, social support provides much-needed emotional support in the face of an anxiety-provoking situation. Interestingly, when given the choice as to who to wait with, participants also chose specifically to wait with people who were also going to take part in the study. This suggests that it was the anxiety about the shared experience that was key to social support in this context.

Misattribution

Experiencing anxiety can not only lead to a desire to affiliate, but can go even further and elicit powerful feelings of sexual attraction. Our experience of emotion is based on two things: physiological arousal *and* our interpretation of the cause of that arousal. This means that when anxious we can sometimes look to others to try to understand our physiological state. In other words, we carry out an attributional process (bringing us back to the processes described in Chapter 2).

Recall that attribution is the process used by the social mind to work out the causes of people's behaviour—whether they are situational or dispositional. This process can operate when we're trying to work out the causes of others people's behaviour, but also our own. When this attributional process is engaged in contexts where we feel anxiety, some interesting effects can be observed.

In a now classic study, Dutton and Aron asked groups of male participants to carry out a survey while crossing a stable rope bridge *or* on a scarily high rope bridge. The participants were asked to create a story about anything they wanted and to write it down. The female researcher who was conducting the study found that the males on the scarily high bridge were more likely to use sexual imagery in the story—and more likely to call her afterwards for 'more details' of the study!

This study shows how people can sometimes misattribute one feeling to another cause—based on what is most salient in the context. Here the male participants misattributed their anxiety at being on a high, swaying rope bridge to sexual arousal for the female researcher.

Although this experiment is about misattribution, it also tells us a lot about how we come to feel that we are in love. When we meet that special someone it has a whole range of physiological effects, many of which are akin to feeling anxiety (heart quickening, butterflies in the stomach, etc.). When it is obvious that our potential paramour is the cause of these feelings it makes it easy for us to attribute our feelings to our burgeoning love for them.

Evolution

A well-establish criterion for physical attractiveness is facial symmetry, which is associated with genetic, physical, and mental health. This provides an evolutionary explanation for why certain people are considered more attractive than others. However, it is difficult to disentangle this explanation from a socially constructed one, i.e. that society has simply prescribed that a particular 'look' is desirable. While it is undoubtedly the case that culture and the media have an influence on what is considered attractive, an intriguing study by Thornhill and Gangestad demonstrates strong support that evolution at least plays a part in the explanation for attractiveness.

The facial symmetry of eighty male participants was measured. They were then given a clean, brand-new cotton shirt and asked to wear it for two nights while sleeping. The shirts were then given back to the researchers who asked female participants to sniff them and rate each one for pleasantness and sexiness. What the researchers found was incredible. Despite having never set eyes on the wearers of the shirts, there was a positive correlation between the female rater's preference and the objectively measured facial symmetry of the shirt's owner. In other words, the women preferred the smell of shirts belonging to men with more symmetrical faces.

Even more interesting, the relationship between shirt-smell preference and facial symmetry only occurred for women who were about to ovulate. From an evolutionary perspective, this suggests that pheromones released by men contain information about their genetic health, and that women at their most fertile become attuned to detect this. Doing so helps increase the chances that any conception will result in the most healthy offspring possible.

Evolutionary processes are also implicated in men's apparent susceptibility to the colour red. Recent research has found that the colour red can lead men to find women more attractive and sexually desirable. Notably, red doesn't seem to make women seem more attractive to women, nor affect other judgement criteria (such as liking or intelligence). This, along with the fact that similar effects have been observed in primates, supports the idea that men's preference for the colour red has an evolutionary origin.

Finally, another evolutionary theory is the principle of *looks-for-exchange*. One survey, carried out across thirty-seven countries, found a pervasive tendency for men to prefer women who are younger and for women to prefer men who are older. From an evolutionary perspective the argument is that women in ancestral habitats sought mates who could provide a safe, well-resourced environment for their offspring. On the other hand, ancestral men sought women who were likely to be of reproductive age and of high genetic health.

However, there is also a socio-cultural explanation. Historically men have held the power and status and women have been objectified, valued only in terms of their physical beauty. While there is some evidence for this trade-off, there is also evidence that the looks-for-exchange phenomenon is changing as society changes (providing stronger support for the socio-cultural explanation). Some studies have found that women under the age of forty are increasingly seeking attractiveness in potential male partners, and that men are no longer only interested in looks but are increasingly seeking women who are successful and have achieved higher social status.

Attachment

Once we are in love, what determines how we act in that relationship and how satisfying it will be? According to *social penetration theory* we start off by gradually revealing more and more intimate details about ourselves to our partner (going from superficial to more in-depth and personal topics of discussion). This slowly builds intimacy. However, if too much is disclosed too quickly, this can feel uncomfortable and the interaction may become stilted, and the relationship even derailed. To avoid this people typically follow the norm of reciprocity (matching each other's level of self-disclosure).

Self-disclosure, from early stages right through the life of the relationship, is one of the things that is determined by our *attachment style*. Attachment theory was originally proposed by John Bowlby in 1969 as a framework for understanding how young infants form bonds with their primary caregiver (usually the mother). The idea was then extended to suggest that people form different attachment styles depending upon the experiences they have with their primary caregiver, and these styles go on to determine how people react to others in relationships in later life, and how they perceive others.

According to the theory, a secure attachment style is developed in children whose caregiver is responsive and sensitive to their needs. An avoidant style is developed when the caregiver does not respond consistently to the child's needs, leading to the child finding it difficult to trust other people in later life. An anxious/ambivalent style is developed when the caregiver shows a disinterest in interacting with the child, leading to a tendency in later life to want intimacy, but to not believe one is worthy of love.

Although whether the attachment style in childhood is transferred to adulthood is disputed (i.e. it may be that adult attachment style develops later in life), the basic framework of different styles do appear to predict relationship behaviour in adulthood. For instance, people who are low on avoidance and low on anxiety are *secure* and said to have high self-esteem and trust others. They have an adaptive relationship style and form relations with ease. Regardless of one's own attachment style, securely attached individuals are the most preferred among all others.

People low on avoidance but high on anxiety are said to be *preoccupied*. While they are positive and trust others, they have low self-esteem and ruminate on their own self-worth. They tend to be self-focused, considering their worth in terms of their physical appearance rather than character traits. They are 'clingy', desiring attention and confirmation that they are loved. They are said to fall in love most easily, perhaps often with the wrong person, and are most likely to be perceived as unhappy.

Dismissing-avoidant style people are high on avoidance and low on anxiety. They are said to have high self-esteem, but find intimacy uncomfortable. They are said to not read emotions in others well, and would rather withdraw from a relationship than work out problems. They are self-reliant and likely to be promiscuous, having a string of shallow relationships. Finally, *fearful avoidant* people are high on anxiety *and* high on avoidance. They are thought to have low self-esteem and don't trust others. Research also suggests that these individuals pick up on angry and sad faces more quickly than other people.

Relationships across the lifespan

What determines whether romantic relationships last, and what happens when they don't? The early stages of love are characterized by what's called *passionate love*—a preoccupation and longing for the other person, accompanied by intense emotions. It is also accompanied by changes in brain chemistry, notably an increase in dopamine production. Interestingly, brain imaging studies have demonstrated that when shown photographs of one's partner (versus one's friends) people show heightened activity in the caudate nucleus—one of the oldest parts of the brain that is associated with reward and pleasure. This supports the idea discussed at the very start of this chapter, that our need for interpersonal relations is hardwired into the very fabric of the social mind.

As relationships develop, passionate love is gradually replaced by *companionate love*. Companionate love is characterized by close personal intimacy, and a sense of being 'at one' with the other person. Companionate love can be empirically measured through the concept of self–other overlap.

Research has shown how people in relationships gradually come to see their own identity as overlapping with their romantic partner's. One study tested couples who had been in a romantic relationship for three months or more. Each partner was asked to say how descriptive ninety personality traits were for both themselves and their romantic partner. The same ninety traits were then presented on a computer screen in random order. Each partner was asked to press 'yes' if the trait on the screen was descriptive of their partner, and 'no' if not. What they found was that participants' responses were significantly faster in identifying a trait their partner possessed if they themselves also possessed it. Furthermore, the closer the romantic relationship, the stronger was the effect.

This methodology and idea is similar to the IAT (see Chapter 4). It suggests that people come to 'confuse' their own traits and characteristics with those of their partner. It is like when people in long-term relationships start to talk about, 'we like this...we like that'. Interestingly, while people who are already similar in terms of attitudes, interests, etc. start off more likely to come together, they also appear to become *more* similar over time. Indeed, one study of married couples over twenty-one years found that over time the couples became increasingly similar.

Finally, couples even tend to *look* more like each other over time. This is thought to be because of shared diet, emotional experiences, living conditions, and lifestyle. One study found that judges rated pictures of married couples who had been together for twenty-five years as more similar to each other than randomly paired control couples.

The investment model

As relationships progress through the lifespan, the longevity and success of the relationship can be predicted based on three criteria, outlined by Rusbult's investment model.

The first criterion is high satisfaction. This is the most obvious—people must gain positive value from the relationship. However, satisfaction can be low and commitment can be high, perhaps counter-intuitively, when the other criteria come into play.

The second criterion is investment. As time goes on partners become increasingly invested in one another emotionally, socially (e.g. shared friends), as well as financially. They may, for instance, make sacrifices for their career for the sake of the relationship. This represents a considerable investment that provides inertia working against dissolution. Recall the discussion of cognitive dissonance in Chapter 3. Avoiding cognitive dissonance is one of the things that glues people together in relationships. Having invested all that time and effort in building a relationship and life together, the idea of leaving the relationship causes an unpleasant feeling of dissonance, so people conclude that they must still be in love with their partner. Maybe this is why many people appear to stay in relationships even when satisfaction is low—the avoidance of a worse negative feeling brought about by cognitive dissonance.

The third criterion is a low perceived quality of alternatives. A dissatisfied partner may believe that they would be unable to find an alternative (perhaps because of low self-esteem, low perceived attractiveness, or age). Or they may believe there are no alternatives available (e.g. before the days of Internet dating people might simply have thought there was no way for them to meet someone else). In these cases commitment can remain high even in a relationship characterized by low satisfaction. The partner may believe that the current relationship is as good as they can get, and that living alone, losing friends, etc. may be too high a cost to pay.

Protecting successful relationships

People in happy, committed relationships also use strategies to protect their relationship from the threat offered by alternative potential partners. These strategies can include derogating attractive alternatives and closing off their partner from the opportunity and appeal of those alternatives. An intriguing study shows how people also unconsciously push away threatening alternatives themselves, thus avoiding even being tempted away from a committed relationship. Research has found that, when asked to converse with an attractive person of the opposite sex, people in committed heterosexual relationships mimicked the attractive interaction partner less (mimicry being a non-verbal indication of attraction). Furthermore, effect was more pronounced the more the participant reported being close to their romantic partner (i.e. really close relationships led to almost no mimicry at all). Both men and women showed the effect, suggesting that mimicry is an unconscious way to signal availability (or unavailability) to potential mates.

Afterword

So that's a very short introduction to social psychology. We've taken a tour of the social mind and seen the profound impact that our relationships have on attitudes, beliefs, and behaviour. Social psychology is there in every interaction, every attitude, every action we take. It tells us why we like some people and dislike others; why we're confident, afraid, elated, and proud. It speaks to the most important issues we face, from immigration to economics to the environment.

Our understanding of the physical universe is profound, detailed, and complex. In contrast, we are only just beginning to understand the inner workings of the social mind, and the intimate and intricate ways in which the atoms of our social universe interact. Social psychology has made such great leaps in the past one hundred years, but there is still so much we don't know. And it is this that makes it one of the most thrilling, engaging, and exciting endeavours of the 21st century.

Further reading

Chapter 1: All about us

Allport, F. H. (1924). *Social psychology*. Boston: Houghton Mifflin.

Le Bon, G. (1885/2002). *The crowd: a study of the popular mind*. New York: Dover Publications.

McDougall, W. (1908/2009). *An introduction to social psychology*. Charleston: BiblioLife.

Chapter 2: The social mind

Bargh, J. A., Chen, M., and Burrows, L. (1996). Automaticity of social behavior: Direct effects of trait construct and stereotype activation on action. *Journal of Personality and Social Psychology*, 71, 230–44.

Fiske, S. T. and Taylor, S. E. (1991). *Social cognition* (2nd edn.). New York: McGraw-Hill.

Heider, F. and Simmel, M. (1944). An experimental study of apparent behavior. *American Journal of Psychology*, 57, 243–59.

Jones, E. E. and Harris, V. A. (1967). The attribution of attitudes. *Journal of Experimental Social Psychology*, 3, 1–24.

Kelley, H. H. and Michela, J. L. (1980). Attribution theory and research. *Annual Review of Psychology*, 31, 457–501.

Storms, M. D. (1973). Videotape and the attribution process: Reversing actors' and observers' points of view. *Journal of Personality and Social Psychology*, 27, 165–75.

Tversky, A. and Kahneman, D. (1974). Judgement under uncertainty: Heuristics and biases. *Science*, 185, 1124–31.

Chapter 3: Attitudes and influence

Asch, S. E. (1956). Opinions and social pressure. *Scientific American*, *193*, 31–5.

Bem, D. J. (1967). Self-perception: An alternative interpretation of cognitive dissonance phenomena. *Psychological Review, 74*, 183–200.

Festinger, L. and Carlsmith, J. M. (1959). Cognitive consequences of forced compliance. *Journal of Abnormal and Social Psychology, 58*, 203–10.

Latané, B., Williams, K., and Harkins, S. (1979). Many hands make light work: The causes and consequences of social loafing. *Journal of Personality and Social Psychology, 37*, 822–32.

Moscovici, S., Lage, E., and Naffrechoux, M. (1969). Influence of a consistent minority on the responses of a majority in a color perception task. *Sociometry, 32*, 365–79.

Petty, R. E. and Cacioppo, J. T. (1986). The elaboration likelihood model of persuasion. In L. Berkowitz (ed.), *Advances in experimental social psychology* (Vol. 19, pp. 123–205). New York: Academic Press.

Sherif, M. (1935). A study of some social factors in perception. *Archives of Psychology, 27*, 187.

Staats, C. K. and Staats, A. W. (1958). Attitudes established by classical conditioning. *Journal of Abnormal and Social Psychology, 57*, 37–40.

Zajonc, R. B. (1968). Attitudinal effects of mere exposure. *Journal of Personality and Social Psychology, 9*, 1–27.

Chapter 4: Obedience, oppression, and aggression

Adorno, T. W., Frenkel-Brunswick, E., Levinson, D. J., and Stanford, R. N. (1950). *The authoritarian personality*. New York: Harper and Row.

Berkowitz, L. (1969). The frustration-aggression hypothesis revisited. In L. Berkowitz (ed.), *Roots of aggression* (pp. 1–28). New York: Atherton Press.

Dollard, J., Doob, L. W., Miller, N. E., Mowrer, O. H., and Sears, R. R. (1939). *Frustration and aggression*. New Haven, CT: Yale University Press.

Greenberg, J., Pyszczynski, T., and Solomon, S. (1986). The causes and consequences of self-esteem: A terror management theory. In R. Baumeister (ed.), *Public self and private self* (pp. 189–212). New York: Springer.

Greenwald, A. G., McGhee, D. E., and Schwartz, J. L. K. (1998).
Measuring individual differences in implicit cognition: The
implicit association test. *Journal of Personality and Social
Psychology*, *74*, 1464–80.

Hamilton, D. L. and Gifford, R. K. (1976). Illusory correlation in
interpersonal personal perception: A cognitive basis of stereotypic
judgements. *Journal of Experimental Social Psychology*, *12*,
392–407.

Hovland, C. I. and Sears, R. R. (1940). Minor studies in aggression:
VI. Correlation of lynchings with economic indices. *Journal of
Psychology*, *9*, 301–10.

Milgram, S. (1963). Behavioral study of obedience. *Journal of
Abnormal and Social Psychology*, *67*, 371–8.

Moghaddam, F. M. (2005). The staircase to terrorism: A psychological
exploration. *American Psychologist*, *60*, 161–9.

Chapter 5: Intergroup relations

Allport, G. W. (1954). *The nature of prejudice*. Reading, MA:
Addison-Wesley.

Cialdini, R. B., Borden, R. J., Thorne, A., Walker, M. R., Freeman, S.,
and Sloan, L. R. (1976). Basking in reflected glory: Three football
field studies. *Journal of Personality and Social Psychology*, *34*,
366–75.

Crisp, R. J. and Turner, R. N. (2009). Can imagined interactions
produce positive perceptions? Reducing prejudice through
simulated social contact. *American Psychologist*, *64*, 231–40.

Gaertner, S. L., Mann, J. A., Murrell, A. J., and Dovidio, J. F. (1989).
Reducing intergroup bias: The benefits of recategorization.
Journal of Personality and Social Psychology, *57*, 239–49.

Sherif, M., White, B. J., and Harvey, O. J. (1955). Status in experimentally
produced groups. *American Journal of Sociology*, *60*, 370–9.

Tajfel, H., Billig, M., Bundy, R., and Flament, C. (1971). Social
categorization and intergroup behaviour. *European Journal of
Social Psychology*, *1*, 149–78.

Chapter 6: Love and other attractions

Bowlby, J. (1969). *Attachment and loss (Vol. 1): Attachment*. London:
Hogarth Press.

Dutton, D. G. and Aron, A. P. (1974). Some evidence for heightened sexual attraction under conditions of high anxiety. *Journal of Personality and Social Psychology*, *28*, 510–17.

Rusbult, C. E. (1983). A longitudinal test of the investment model: The development (and deterioration) of satisfaction and commitment in heterosexual involvements. *Journal of Personality and Social Psychology*, *45*, 101–17.

Thornhill, R. and Gangestad, S. W. (1999). The scent of symmetry: A human pheromone that signals fitness? *Evolution and Human Behavior*, *20*, 175–201.

Williams, K. D. and Jarvis, B. (2006). Cyberball: A program for use in research on interpersonal ostracism and acceptance. *Behavior Research Methods, Instruments, and Computers*, *38*, 174–80.

Index

Expand your collection of
VERY SHORT INTRODUCTIONS